ABOUT ISLAND PRESS

Island Press is the only nonprofit organization in the United States whose principal purpose is the publication of books on environmental issues and natural resource management. We provide solutions-oriented information to professionals, public officials, business and community leaders, and concerned citizens who are shaping responses to environmental problems.

In 1998, Island Press celebrates its fourteenth anniversary as the leading provider of timely and practical books that take a multidisciplinary approach to critical environmental concerns. Our growing list of titles reflects our commitment to bringing the best of an expanding body of literature to the environmental community throughout North America and the world.

Support for Island Press is provided by The Jenifer Altman Foundation, The Bullitt Foundation, The Mary Flagler Cary Charitable Trust, The Nathan Cummings Foundation, The Geraldine R. Dodge Foundation, The Ford Foundation, The Vira I. Heinz Endowment, The W. Alton Jones Foundation, The John D. and Catherine T. MacArthur Foundation, The Andrew W. Mellon Foundation, The Curtis and Edith Munson Foundation, The National Fish and Wildlife Foundation, The National Science Foundation, The New-Land Foundation, The David and Lucile Packard Foundation, The Surdna Foundation, The Winslow Foundation, The Pew Charitable Trusts, and individual donors.

With People in Mind

*To the many individuals in our far-flung academic
family whose research made this book possible.*

With People in Mind
Design and Management of Everyday Nature

Rachel Kaplan, Stephen Kaplan,
and Robert L. Ryan

ISLAND PRESS

Washington, D.C. • Covelo, California

Kaplan, Rachel.
      With People in mind : design and management of everyday nature/
Rachel Kaplan, Stephen Kaplan, and Robert L. Ryan.
              p.   cm.
      Includes bibliographical references and index.
      ISBN 1-55963-594-0 (paper)
      1. Human beings—Effect of environment on.   2. Environmental
psychology.   3. Environmental management.   I. Kaplan, Stephen,
1936–   . II. Ryan, Robert L.   III. Title.
GF51.K37   1998
333.78'215—dc21
                                                                    97-49586
                                                                    CIP

Printed on recycled, acid-free paper ✸

Manufactured in the United States of America

10 9 8 7 6 5 4 3 2 1

Contents

Preface   *ix*

Acknowledgments   *xiii*

Part I By Way of Explanation: People and Nature   1

Chapter 1   The Use of Patterns   3

Chapter 2   Some Human Characteristics   7

Part II Meeting the Challenges   29

Chapter 3   Fears and Preferences   31

Chapter 4   Way-finding   49

Chapter 5   Restorative Environments   67

Part III Design and Management Opportunities   79

Chapter 6   Gateways and Partitions   81

Chapter 7   Trails and Locomotion   89

Chapter 8   Views and Vistas   99

Chapter 9   Places and Their Elements   109

Part IV With People in Mind   121

Chapter 10   Engaging People   123

Chapter 11   Putting It Together   147

Appendix: Matrix of Patterns and Themes   163

Readings: By Subject   167

Readings: Alphabetic   195

Photo Credits   217

Index   219

Preface

When we began studying the relationship between people and nature over twenty-five years ago, we found little research that addressed this topic. It was not known whether people prefer natural environments to other settings. (They do.) Nor was it known if there were other benefits beyond the mere fact of enjoyment. (There are.) We began doing research in this area with two hopes, namely, that there would be orderly enough patterns to make scientific research possible, and that the results would have a beneficial effect on the design and management of the natural landscape.

The first hope has been realized. Although we were warned that there is too much idiosyncrasy to find regularities, that has not been the case. The body of research addressing issues related to people and the natural environment has grown substantially; by now it is clear that findings in this area show a great deal of stability and consistency.

In our second hope, however, we were not as fortunate. When we look around us, there are some excellent examples of design and management of natural areas that keep people in mind. Unfortunately, there are also numerous examples that show no hint of putting the research findings into practice. Although disappointing, this is hardly surprising. There has not been an easy way to access the research literature and translate it into usable recommendations.

This book is an effort to address that gap. We have tried to organize and summarize the research carried out by us, our students and former students, their students, and other colleagues in a simple, direct, and practical way. The book means to be readable, useful, and flexible. It is not an exhaustive treatise but rather a sampling of issues that are pervasive in many situations and contexts. It is more oriented to participation than to final solutions, more focused on small spaces than large ones, and more about the psychological dimensions of having nature nearby than about detailed, site-specific considerations. Our intention was to be guided by theory and by research, to focus on the people aspects, and to use a framework that encourages the reader to try things out.

We had diverse audiences in mind in preparing this material: individuals who have a stake in or responsibility for the design and management of parks, preserves, corporate landscapes, and many other kinds of nearby natural settings. Such individuals come with a wide range of expertise and training. Many have more knowledge of the ecosystem requirements of the environment than of the needs and inclinations of the people who will be nurtured by and, in turn, help to nurture these places. Others may have more knowledge of architectural and design theory than of research that can provide grounding for their intuitions. Still others may have studied some of the themes we cover but have asked for a coherent format for using the information.

We hope all these individuals will benefit from the distillation of a great deal of research, from having a conceptual framework, and from the concrete recommendations. Furthermore, it is our hope that readers will find it useful to have a justification for what they may already be doing, namely, designing and managing natural areas in ways that benefit the tranquillity, the reasonableness, and the effectiveness of the people who come in contact with them.

The three of us have played very different roles in the shaping of this book. While Rachel Kaplan and Stephen Kaplan have for a while been a writing and research team, their specific contributions to the volume can be distinguished. Stephen Kaplan was the major force behind the conceptual framework and the application of the "pattern" approach to the book, while Rachel Kaplan did most of the writing and translation of theory and research results into patterns. The third member of the team, Robert L. Ryan, was responsible for the graphics and captions, including drawing the sketches, taking many of the photographs, and selecting the other illustrations. In addition, he was the primary force in preparing the extensive bibliographic section. In the final analysis, however, the book has been a collaborative venture, with each of us benefiting from the others' comments and feedback.

As was true with our previous books, our involvement with this volume is conceptual and moral rather than financial. To receive the royalties this time, we sought an organization that was involved with the preservation of environments that would benefit and be appreciated by people. We are delighted to have found an inspiring and appropriate organization in the Trust for Public Land. We are greatly impressed by TPL's flexibility and ingenuity, and we are heartened to find an organization that shares our focus on everyday nature and on the importance of these settings for people. In an interview with Susan Ives for *Land and People* magazine, Martin J. Rosen, TPL president, captured this spirit beautifully in a few words:

> It is not just sensational or extraordinary landscapes—the Yosemites and Grand Canyons—that deserve respect and protection. We rec-

ognize the importance of ordinary, close-at-hand landscapes. The pond in your neighborhood may not be as famous as Walden Pond, or your local waterfall may not be Niagara Falls, but these places nourish us on a daily basis.

Acknowledgments

The adventure that led to this book started quite a few years ago and involves a debt of gratitude to John F. Dwyer. As project leader of the Chicago Urban Forestry Unit of the North Central Forest Experiment Station, USDA Forest Service, John Dwyer played a central role not only through financial support of this project and many that are reflected in it, but also through his enthusiasm and encouragement over a long period of time.

In many parts of the book we emphasize our commitment to incorporating input from those who will be impacted by the results. We took the same approach in writing the book. We benefited enormously from the feedback of our many reviewers. Many of these are practitioners, as indicated by their job titles: manager of a state recreation area, coordinator of nature and interpretive services at the county level, district landscape architect for a metropark system, assistant director of parks and community services in a metropolitan area, coordinator of natural area preservation for a city, capital resources director for a municipal parks and recreation department, director of a nonprofit environment preservation agency for a large city, and principal of a firm specializing in graphics and way-finding. Also included were individuals whose primary job is academic (landscape architecture, recreation, environmental planning, and forest resources) or research (social science research for the U.S. Forest Service and management of research and program evaluation for a metropark system). The reviewers represented diverse geographical areas, including the Northwest, the East, and several Great Lakes states.

We wish to thank the anonymous reviewers of the book as well as the many individuals who commented on portions of earlier versions of the manuscript or reviewed the entire draft document: David Borneman, Gordon Bradley, Gerald Clark, John Cardwell, Cynthia Carlisle, Jennifer Colby, Jeff Corbin, Jeff Dehring, Kathy Dickhut, Luci Fortin, Paul H. Gobster, Robert E. Grese, William E. Hammitt, Matthew C. Heumann, Roger Hoesterey, Jon P. LaBossiere, Rookie Riegler, Thomas Stanley, Andy Stone, and William C. Sullivan. We especially appreciate Robert Bixler's extensive, far-reaching, and thoughtful comments. In addition, the contributions of Maureen Austin, Thomas Herzog, and Janet Talbot are greatly appreciated.

We wish to thank also the many people whose illustrations have been included in the volume. Specific credits are listed in the back of the book. We appreciate the patience, skill, and attention to detail of D. C. Goings and the staff at the University of Michigan Campus and Photo Services. And a special thanks to Janet Ryan for her patience and participation in countless photographic expeditions.

Finally, our work has benefited from the insights and perceptive questions of many generations of students and colleagues as well as individuals in the audience in places near and far. We have had the good fortune to work with many dozens of superb students and to be involved in the research efforts of their students as well. The book reflects what we have gained from the wisdom and understanding of many others.

Part I

By Way of Explanation: People and Nature

This book is about nature, but it is also about people. It is about the way the natural environment can foster well-being and can enhance people's ability to function effectively. The underlying purpose of the book is to explore the design and management of nearby natural areas in ways that are beneficial for people and appreciated by them.

This brief overview signals that the book's perspective, as its title indicates, is "with people in mind." It also signals that we use the word "nature" broadly. There are a good many conflicting perspectives on what constitutes nature. Those, in turn, lead to differing views of the desirable relationship between people and the natural environment.

From our perspective, the natural environment is not characterized by its distance from human settlement. Nor is a natural area necessarily one that is unaltered by human intervention. We use the word nature to include a great variety of outdoor settings that have substantial amounts of vegetation. The focus is on the setting rather than the plants themselves, and on flora rather than fauna. The settings we emphasize are not the wild and awesome, distant and dramatic, lush and splendid. Rather, the emphasis is on the everyday, often unspectacular, natural environment that is, or ideally would be, nearby. That includes parks and open spaces, street trees, vacant lots, and backyard gardens, as well as fields and forests. Included are places that range from tiny to quite large, from visible through the window to more distant, from carefully managed to relatively neglected. The justification for this broad view is neither a personal whim nor an ideological stance. Rather, it is based on what we have learned from a great deal of research. We have found repeatedly that people's concept of nature is broad and inclusive. We have also found that the kinds of natural settings that are beneficial to human well-being include a great diversity.

1

We see people as a part of the natural world. People, like all other creatures, have needs; their health is influenced by how well those needs are met. The process of meeting those needs impacts the environment. That is true for all living things.

It is also true that humans have transformed the environment, natural and otherwise, with dire consequences to all living things. What was once undisturbed nature is no longer to be found. What was once a healthy environment for other plants and animals is now often degraded. What was once a healthy place for humans has suffered as well.

Given the damage that we humans have caused, there is understandably a widely shared feeling that correcting things should have high priority. Some professionals consider it far more important to emphasize educating the public about ecosystem requirements than to cater to what they see as endless and costly human desires. We are inclined to seek a middle ground. Needless to say, our purpose is not to encourage further deterioration of the natural environment, even in the urban and near-urban settings that are central to our focus. It is our hope that many of those areas can be improved ecologically in the process of benefiting people.

At the same time we must admit to having reservations about "educating the public" as a sufficient approach to the people–nature problem. We are not opposed to education, but we are aware of how difficult a process it is. Even if education were straightforward, there is the issue of who has the "right" answers. Too often, the underlying assumption in the "educate-the-public" stance is that those with the message, the experts, have the appropriate solution and those who are to receive the message, the public, are ignorant. As will be evident in many parts of this book, and especially in the final section, we consider the public to have pertinent insights and information that experts need to hear.

The intent of this book, then, is to focus on the role of everyday nature in the well-being of everyday people. The approach of the book is based both on research and on a conceptual framework that grew out of that research. It is our conviction that everyday nature can make a significant contribution to people's everyday lives. Nearby nature can foster well-being. Nature views have been demonstrated to be related to greater physical and mental health. Activities that are nature-related have been shown to help people go about their lives more effectively.

Chapter 1

The Use of Patterns

The book is intended to be practical and useful. It is organized around themes and problems that occur in many situations. Each of these is the topic of a chapter, and each such chapter contains a series of "patterns" that offer a way of thinking about the problem. The patterns are not formulas. Rather their purpose is to suggest a relationship between aspects of the environment and how people experience or react to them. These relationships form the basis for recommendations or possible solutions to recurring situations. The possible solutions we offer are far from exhaustive; they are meant to inform and inspire, not to dictate. There is rarely a solution that is universal. Rather, the "correct" solution, in our view, is one that is locally appropriate and responsive to the situation at hand. An approach that is sensitive to people's inclinations is less likely to be identically applicable in different settings.

The notion of patterns comes from the work of Christopher Alexander and his coauthors (1977). They characterize this approach in the following words: "Each pattern describes a problem which occurs over and over again in our environment, and then describes the core of the solution to that problem, in such a way that you can use this solution a million times over, without ever doing it the same way twice" (p. x).

The pattern concept can usefully be contrasted with the idea of a rule. A rule indicates what is to be done in a given situation. A pattern raises issues that may need attention and provides ideas and examples of what could be done to address them. Thus, while a rule bypasses people's intuitions, a pattern calls upon these intuitions and attempts to educate and strengthen them in the process of solving the problem.

The forty-five patterns in this book have been chosen to highlight a set of issues that we consider particularly important in the context of a people-oriented approach to the design and management of natural environments. These issues are not discrete or isolated; thus the appropriate combination of patterns will vary with the circumstances. The patterns have been given unique codes, designating their general thematic area. For example, patterns related to views and vistas start with "VV" while those related to way-finding have "WF" designations. In putting them to use, it is likely that several patterns within the same family (sharing the same initial) will be pertinent. Solutions to many problems, however, will also benefit from patterns in other chapters. The list of all the patterns in the "Matrix of Patterns and Themes" at the end of the book provides a quick checklist of issues to consider when attempting to incorporate a people perspective. Once again, we want to emphasize that the patterns are meant to be guiding and flexible. They are not recipes, nor do they come with promises of perfect outcomes.

We have tried to limit our focus, by and large, to topics that can be guided by the research literature concerning people and nature. A major purpose of looking to research for answers is as a check on intuitions. The expert's way of seeing is often different from the public's. "Experts" here includes those with professional training (for example, in natural resources, landscape architecture, environmental education, or park administration), as well as those whose knowledge has come from informal learning (for example, long-term volunteers in stewardship programs or members of wildflower clubs). Such individuals have repeatedly been shown to have different perceptions and different preferences of the natural environment than the rest of the population. If one is designing for the public, one's own experiences and insights are unlikely to be sufficient.

The research we draw on was carried out by a great many people in numerous places over an extended period of time. We also draw on a conceptual framework that grew from the results of the research. However, to keep the book from becoming a scholastic rather than a practical volume, the references are generally not cited in the text. Instead, the final section of the book provides an extensive bibliography to those published works. These readings are presented both alphabetically and by subject. The "Readings by Subject" listing begins with citations to general references that pertain to many portions of the volume. Subsequently, the readings are organized to correspond to each of the chapters of the book.

Many ideological and political conflicts related to the issues raised by this book could in principle be profitably addressed by research. It would be helpful, for example, to show that people who find parks and forests comfortable to be in and agreeable to look at are more likely to support an agenda for ecological restoration. It would be powerful to be able to show that public expenditure aimed at reducing crime and improving mental health could be offset by increasing attention to the design and management of everyday nature. It would also be valuable to show that efforts to educate the public are more likely to have the desired results if they are based on understanding people's needs and inclinations. Unfortunately, here as in many other areas of application, the research that would ideally guide one's actions is yet to be done. Until more data are available on these topics, they have to be considered as no more than theoretically reasonable hypotheses.

Overview and How to Use the Book

We are committed to the notion that although people are different in many important respects, they also have some shared needs. That perspective is basic to the content of this book.

By the same token, there is not a right way to use this book. A few readers will begin at the start and continue in sequence. Many others are likely to turn to specific chapters as the design or management of a particular situation motivates their search. The framework that guides the book can be found in chapter 2, "Some Human Characteristics."

The chapters in the rest of the book focus on patterns. Each set of patterns is oriented around a common theme, such as way-finding, trails, or participation. Such an organization is useful, but it may also deceive in its simplicity. The design of trails, for example, is likely to entail way-finding concerns and way-finding concerns are more likely to be resolved with participation. As mentioned earlier, the intention of patterns is that they be used in combination.

The themes containing the patterns form the heart of the book. Each of these begins with an introduction that highlights key issues that the patterns in that chapter address, provides an overview of the basis for these patterns, and concludes with a listing of the patterns in that chapter.

As mentioned, each pattern has been given an identifying code consisting of initials designating the theme and a number. The patterns in the Restorative Environments chapter, for example, are numbered R1 to R5. Each pattern has a brief title to highlight its focus. For example, R1 is called "Quiet Fascination." This is followed by a concise statement summarizing the intention of the pattern. Each pattern is then presented through text and graphics, which are intended to jointly provide imagery about the kinds of solutions the pattern might entail.

The themes are grouped into three major sections. Part II discusses some psychological concerns that arise in many settings. The first of its three chapters addresses ways to create environments that are responsive to people's preferences and that reduce their fears. It explores how natural settings can be more comfortable and satisfying by focusing on physical aspects of the settings. The second chapter concerns ways to facilitate finding one's way into a natural area, within it, and back out again. Getting lost, or worrying about getting lost, is not a preferred state. Yet the design and management of many natural settings fail to address people's concerns about finding their way. The final chapter in this section deals with creating opportunities for people to restore themselves, to recover from the wear and tear of daily demands. Natural settings are often sought for their restorative capabilities. We offer some patterns for enhancing that vital function.

Part III is organized around some landscape elements that are particularly important for making environments supportive of people's needs. Entrances, or "gateways," are the focus of the first chapter. While a gateway is part of its environment, it serves the psychologically important function of providing the user information about what lies ahead. The second chapter, on trails, includes patterns that make moving through an area a satisfying activity. The third chapter deals with enhancing views and vistas, situations where a natural environment might be experienced from a distance. The final chapter in part III, "Places and Their Elements," considers factors that strongly influence people's preferences, such as trees and water, as well as the size and feel of enclosures.

The two chapters in the final portion of the book repeat many of the themes that were discussed previously. The first explores some remedies for problems that frequently accompany expertise. The patterns here focus on ways to make the participation and involvement of the users of a setting more likely and more satisfying, so that the unique strengths of the experts and the public can be brought together. The concluding chapter revisits the forty-five patterns in the context of four overarching themes. It shows how the building blocks represented by the various patterns can be combined in different ways and in a variety of contexts.

It is our hope that readers will try some of the ideas and suggestions presented in these pages to see how they work in the context of their particular settings. Taking such an exploratory approach is the recommendation of the last of the patterns, "Small Experiments." Its intention is to encourage an adventurous attitude and a willingness to proceed in small steps. By being sensitive to outcomes, efforts that did not work need not be seen as disasters, but rather as stepping stones along the path to good decisions.

Chapter 2

Some Human Characteristics

This is intended to be a practical book for practical people. Why, then, a chapter on human characteristics? Why not get on with the useful part? Here are some answers:

- Our research and the research of others have made one fact all too clear: Environments are designed and modified every day in ways that fail to support people's needs and requirements.

- Much of this failure is the result of efforts by well-intended individuals who are apparently unaware of certain key aspects of what people find reasonable and appropriate.

- Several of these human needs and requirements are easily identified and discussed.

The intent of this chapter, then, is to look at some specific human characteristics that are central to the design and management of natural settings. The framework developed in this chapter provides the basis for what follows. Here the material is more conceptual; in the rest of the book it is more practical.

Central to the framework is the notion of information. Far more basic than money, information is what really drives our world. And this is not a recent development. Information—about family, making a living, food supply, dangers, and opportunities—has been central to human experience and survival throughout the course of human evolution. Information is central to our effectiveness, to our sense of esteem, to our interdependencies, to the basis for distinguishing ourselves from others—for better or worse. In the sense we are using it here, information is inescapable, essential, and pervasive.

This chapter focuses on three areas.

1. **Information: Understanding and exploration.** First we look at the basic needs people have to understand their surroundings and to have

7

opportunities for exploration. Meeting those needs goes a long way toward providing environments that are supportive of people's inclinations.

2. **The psychological costs of managing information.** This involves the human inclination to do oneself in. More accurately, much of what we do requires concerted effort, and that leads to mental fatigue. Recovering from such fatigue can be greatly facilitated by the way natural settings are designed and managed.

3. **Sharing information.** Exchanging information is central to human functioning. Although we all do it all the time, it is a process fraught with challenges that can be more easily addressed by considering the mental maps of the targeted recipients of the information. But it is difficult to appreciate just how different other people's internal maps are from our own. Recognizing that differences are unavoidable makes it essential that various viewpoints be included in the design and management of everyone's nearby natural environment.

Information: Understanding and Exploration

People depend on information from many sources: friends and family, publications, television and other media, formal education, and, especially, observation. The immediate environment is rich in information that we rely on all the time. Some of the information is urgent and requires action; some seems urgent by its size, movement, or color, making it difficult to ignore even if it is irrelevant to what we are doing.

In addition to the vast amount of information that surrounds us, there is an enormous amount of information stored in our heads. We can close our eyes and imagine places, we can talk about information that is not directly in front of us, and we can consider alternative plans. These activities all require information that is not immediately present in the environment.

Chaotic environments overwhelm our ability to discern which information is relevant.

Any parent knows just how urgent some information can be for small children.

Storing, using, and evaluating information are basic to human functioning. We humans are addicted to information: we crave it—even when having it makes little difference, we hide it from each other, we peddle it, we keep creating more of it although we do not know what to do with what we already have. In addition, we have strong feelings about it. We use it to judge both the current situation and future possibilities with respect to their being good or bad, pleasant or painful.

The Environment as a Source of Information

The environment provides information in many ways. Clearly, verbal or picture signs, such as stop signs, traffic lights, animal crossings, and the icons at expressway exits are sources of information. People in the environment are also sources of information,

whether we speak to them or not. A large gathering of people would lead to a different interpretation at a supermarket checkout or in a stadium. But even without words or icons and with no people in sight, the environment conveys information.

Much of the information in the environment is related to the things in it—the houses, streets, cars, gardens, trees, forests, ponds. These contents are important to the way a setting is described and to its purposes. A park setting that has benches or play equipment suggests a different kind of park from one that has equestrian trails or a lodge. A lake also would make a difference, and the presence of a fountain in the lake would suggest yet another kind of setting.

Places, however, entail more than their contents. Even a lengthy description of the contents of a particular place would fail to communicate what the place is like. The information in an environment derives not only from its contents but also from its organization. How the contents or elements in an environment are organized can make a significant difference in people's ability to pursue their basic needs of *understanding* and *exploration*. These concepts are at the core of many of the patterns presented in later chapters.

An environment is defined by its contents and their organization.

Understanding refers to the desire people have to make sense of their world, to comprehend what goes on around them. Understanding provides a sense of security. When people cannot understand a situation, they can become distressed. Understanding, however, is not enough. People want to explore, to expand their horizons and find out what lies ahead. They seek more information and look for new challenges. A world without opportunities to explore would be a grim place indeed. Yet, in many settings, such opportunities are severely limited. The combination of those two factors—understanding and exploration—is the basis for the framework that guides many of the recommendations made throughout this book.

The Framework

The understanding-and-exploration framework provides insight into the design and management of the natural environment. This way of think-

ing about places developed from our research on environmental preferences (see "Readings"). The research relies on photographs and slides of
many different places. We ask people to look briefly at each scene and
indicate how much they like it, using a five-point rating scale. Based on
dozens of studies, in many settings, using hundreds of scenes and thousands of such ratings, we learned that what people indicate they like has
a great deal to do with how the space in the picture is organized. They
seem to look at a picture and make a very rapid judgment about how
well they understand it, and how they would feel if they were in that
space—would they feel safe, lost, intrigued?

Scenes that are low in preference. Despite different localities and a
variety of backgrounds, people show remarkable similarities in their ratings of some scenes. Here are two types of settings that consistently
receive low ratings:

Large expanses of undifferentiated landcovers. Even though expanses
of farmland and marshes have different contents, the visual impression
of the way the spaces are organized is similar. They are large areas with
little to focus on. A quick reading of such landscapes, especially for the
novice, suggests that nothing is going on. The apparent sameness of the
landscape indicates that it might be difficult to keep one's bearings. In
addition, one is not enticed to explore the setting because it seems like
it's all the same anyway.

Large expanses of undifferentiated landcovers.

Dense vegetation and obstructed views. Here, too, the contents can be
quite different—for example, a dense forest plantation or a roadside
berm. While the spatial configuration of these settings is totally different
from the wide, open expanses of the previous ones, this kind of scene

also lacks a clear focus and could lead to a concern about becoming lost. For many people, a quick look at these scenes suggests confusion. It is difficult to tell what to expect because the view is blocked.

Dense vegetation and obstructed views.

Scenes that are high in preference. Here again, across many studies that used slides or photographs of entirely different places and participants with diverse experiences, some kinds of settings seem to be highly desirable.

Spaced trees and smooth ground. The trees in these settings may vary in number, height, girth, canopy, and species. The ground may be mowed, grazed, covered with pine needles, or some other relatively smooth surface. The combination, however, leads to a spatial configuration that seems to be highly favored. Such settings offer a strong contrast to both the large expanses and the obstructed views. Here the trees provide a clear focus, and the setting seems to invite entry.

By examining the results of the various studies, looking at many

Spaced trees and smooth ground.

scenes in light of the preference ratings, and considering the issue of how the environment conveys information, we came up with an approach that has been helpful in the design and management of natural settings. This approach involves further dividing understanding and exploration in terms of whether the information extracted from the scene depends on a two-dimensional or a three-dimensional view.

This distinction may seem confusing as a photograph is, of course, two-dimensional. We are referring, however, to the way people perceive and interpret images. The "picture plane" or two-dimensional pattern represents the "surface" of the picture. At a primary level, perception involves a very rapid assessment of the patterns of light and dark. Elements and textures in the scene, including their grouping and location, are extracted from this more primary information. The three-dimensional aspects involve the inference of what is deeper in the scene, despite the fact that the actual image is on a flat surface. This inference about the third dimension occurs rapidly and unconsciously, although it may take a few milliseconds longer than the very rapid processing of the two-dimensional aspects.

Preference Matrix

	UNDERSTANDING	EXPLORATION
2-D	Coherence 連貫性	Complexity
3-D	Legibility 易讀性	Mystery

Of these four informational factors coherence and complexity are based on the two-dimensional plane. They both involve the direct perception of the elements in the scene in terms of their number, grouping, and placement. Legibility and mystery, by contrast, require the inference of the third dimension. When viewing scenes, people not only infer a third dimension, but imagine themselves in the scene. These two factors involve the inference of what being in the pictured space would entail.

As the table further indicates, coherence and legibility share in common that they provide information that can help with making sense of the environment. An environment that is well organized and distinctive is easier to understand. Complexity and mystery, by contrast, concern information that suggests the potential for exploration, either because of the variety of the elements or because of the cues that imply there may be more to be seen. Although in the context of a scene or environment the four informational factors operate jointly, for purposes of explanation, it is useful to consider them one at a time.

Coherence: A coherent setting is orderly; it is organized into clear areas. People can readily discern the presence of a few distinct regions or areas, and those make it easier to make sense of, or understand, a place. Coherence can be increased by having some repeating themes and unifying textures. A limited number of contrasting textures is also helpful. The two scenes in the following figure are similar in terms of the kinds and numbers of different elements, but they differ markedly in terms of coherence. The organization of the scene on the left makes it easier to understand. The scene on the right looks like there is a lot of stuff and little order.

High-coherence scene at left, and low-coherence scene at right.

Complexity: The low-coherence scene (at right) could be used as an example of high complexity. One can readily tell that there is a richness of elements in the setting. It appears intricate, having many different visual components to consider. By contrast, large, open expanses (see photos on p. 11) are low in complexity. Greater richness or variety in such landscapes would encourage exploration.

A popular view of complexity is that too little is boring but too much is overwhelming. We don't agree with that position because we think it is based on confusion between *coherence* and *complexity*. It is all too easy to sacrifice coherence in a highly complex setting. Consider again the two examples in the figure above. The apparent abundance of complexity in the sketch at the right is closely related to its lack of coherence. There is no reason, however, that a highly coherent setting cannot also be very complex. One could imagine, for instance, the sketch at the left made even more complex by the addition of rich textures without compromising its coherence, as shown below.

High complexity and still coherent.

Legibility: The important issue in considering legibility is distinctiveness. To increase legibility, a scene has to have some memorable components that help with orientation. In a legible place, one can imagine finding one's way, not only to a destination but back again as well. A single landmark or an area that is distinctive makes way-finding much more straightforward. Think about a complex trail pattern and what it takes to feel confident that one can retrace one's steps. One may think that a particular pattern of vegetation and paths is distinctive only to discover a little later that other spots look much the same.

What constitutes distinctiveness can be a tricky issue. The awesome, windswept conifer may seem to be a good feature to remember, until one passes the third or fourth or fifth awesome, windswept conifer. Without experience of a place, its unique aspects are difficult to recognize. Experience can make a substantial difference. With familiarity one learns to distinguish patterns in what seemed to be disorder. What at first seems to be an unexciting, undifferentiated area, can, in time, become rich in special features and memorable distinctiveness.

While a single pine tree along a trail is distinctive, one pine tree among many quickly loses its distinctiveness.

What at first appears as an undifferentiated and monotonous area, may in time reveal incredible richness.

Mystery: The desire to explore a place is greatly enhanced if there is some promise that one can find out more as one keeps going. The suggestion that there is more to see is very compelling. There are various ways that the landscape provides hints of what is coming: A curved path is often more enticing than a straight one. Vegetation that partially obscures what lies behind can invite the visitor to take a look. Blocked views (see photos on p. 12, top), however, certainly lack any sense of mystery. When one cannot see anything behind a jumble of vegetation, one is less likely to be intrigued. The various studies of people's preferences for different environments showed that mystery was a particularly effective factor in making a scene highly favored.

Mystery can be a curving path.

Summary

Even small amounts of coherence, legibility, complexity, or mystery can make a substantial difference in how comfortable people feel in a place. Yet many settings lack even minimal amounts of these qualities. The understanding-and-exploration framework and the powerful role of these four informational factors provide the basis for many of the suggestions that are offered in later portions of the book. Information is central to the way people can relate to the environment; it needs also to be central in the way environments are designed and managed.

The Psychological Costs of Managing Information

People have a love–hate relationship with information. We can't survive without it, but there are times we think we can't survive with it, either. Our lives are inundated with information. Some of it is vital. Some is trivial. Some is not important, but the messengers are doing everything in their power to make us think otherwise. Unfortunately, sorting through the information comes at a price. Worse yet, the price is largely invisible.

The informational toll is paid in attention and effort. Struggling to screen out a nearby conversation while focusing on a difficult task is a familiar challenge. Forcing oneself to listen to a friend's tale of woe is another. Sometimes the attentional challenge comes from trying to work despite the disturbing thoughts or worries running around in one's head. And some tasks are inherently difficult, requiring juggling of so many aspects or issues, that maintaining focus is a constant challenge. All these examples require that one concentrate, or focus one's attention. People's capacity for such directed attention is limited. Even if the work that needs to be done is enjoyable and important and one wants to do it, one can only spend so long at it without needing a break. In other words, the capacity to direct attention wears one down. This is a situation we refer to as *mental fatigue*.

Mental fatigue expresses itself in many ways. Having difficulty focusing on the needed work is a clear symptom and becomes problematic as one's attention shifts easily to all the other events and demands in one's immediate environment or in one's head. Other consequences of mental fatigue are expressed in one's actions. One is more likely to take risks, be impulsive and impatient. Irritability is another common symptom. In other words, when attention wears thin, there are many repercussions above and beyond the failures of performing needed tasks. People who are in this state have difficulty taking in information, are more likely to make errors, and are less likely to be decent and helpful to their fellows.

And who hasn't been mentally fatigued? It is not at all unusual for people to go home at the end of the day in something less than a pleasant mood, feeling tired and ornery. Being mentally fatigued, however, does not preclude doing something that is physically demanding. Though one feels tired, the tiredness is related to the need to focus attention. In fact, one is not too tired to do certain kinds of activities.

Doable Activities When Mentally Fatigued

The list of things that are easy to do when one is mentally fatigued is very long. It includes activities that are fun, exciting, fascinating, and transforming. In fact, some activities would be hard not to do because

they are so compelling. For many people a fire, whether on a camping trip or in the fireplace, provides a good example. Many people also find settings that are tranquil and serene to be particularly compelling and absorbing. Some passive involvements in natural settings include: noticing different colors in fall leaves, listening to the wind, watching the clouds go by, and delighting in the antics of a chipmunk.

In contrast to the requirements of directed attention, fascination involves attention that does not demand effort. Something that is fascinating is hard to resist noticing or participating in. One of the important benefits of fascinating situations is that they provide time to recover from mental fatigue. In other words, mental fatigue can be reduced by being in settings that offer fascination. Collecting firewood, walking in the woods, rock climbing, and white water canoeing are all sources of fascination.

That is the simple version of the story. The fuller story is about the various ways to recover from mental fatigue and the characteristics of settings that can facilitate that. While fascination is an important component of recovering from mental fatigue, all fascinations are not equally effective, nor is fascination all that is needed for restoration.

Characteristics of Restorative Settings

The concept of restorative experiences arose in the context of a research program in the wilderness (Kaplan and Kaplan 1989). Fortunately, however, it does not require an intensive nine-day wilderness experience to recover from mental fatigue. In fact, restoration can happen at many different levels and in vastly different amounts of time. Many activities and settings can provide opportunities to recover from mental fatigue. It is striking, however, how readily nature settings and activities that involve the natural environment lend themselves to restoration. Though experiences may differ in scale, they have some properties in common.

These properties are interesting in that they concern both the physical and the mental world at the same time. As conceptual thinkers, people are very good at imagining themselves going places and doing things. Those thoughts can help in the restorative process. Thus, in discussing the characteristics of restorative settings we will be dealing with the rich possibilities created by the combination of real places and places represented by the mind's eye.

Being away. Recovering from mental fatigue requires that one be some place other than the source of the fatigue. People often talk of having to get away, of needing a change. Such expressions indicate accumulated mental fatigue. While people usually think of a physical change in place, getting away can also be achieved more conceptually. Often the mind wanders off to distant places for a moment, while looking out a window, for example. At least for that moment, one can feel that one is far away.

Looking out a window can be restorative, while a meeting is unlikely to be.

Not just any "away" will do when one needs a change. Not infrequently places that are physically distant from one's usual setting contribute to mental fatigue rather than restoring it. Attending a conference, even if its location is an attraction, provides an example of an away that is unlikely to help.

Extent. One reason that some settings are not restorative despite being away is that they are limited in scope or extent. Restorative settings are often described as being a whole different world. There are many ways to accomplish such a sense of being in a large enough place that its boundaries are not evident. A zoo that is designed as a total-immersion experience offers an example of a place that seems to have great extent (a "real" rain forest or savanna). Visitors in such a setting can feel as though they are somewhere that is very different, that has its own rules and properties.

A well-designed zoo exhibit has extent.

Extent can also be created in the mind, influenced by both knowledge and fantasy. Some find a whole world in a slide viewed under a microscope; others find their different world between the covers of a good book. The restorative process can draw upon the remarkable conceptual capacity to elaborate or even transcend what we perceive.

Nature can give a sense of extent, even if one is not in a wilderness. For many people a home garden has extent both in the physical sense and conceptually. Even in the depth of winter, in one's mind one can wander around the garden and consider changes to be made come spring.

Wilderness provides extent, and so does a garden.

Fascination. As we have already mentioned, the experience of fascination is central to giving fatigued attention a rest. A prison cell provides an example of a place that is "away" but hardly qualifies as having either extent or fascination. This example might seem strange, since no one would think of vacationing in a prison cell. "Being away," however, means precisely that. It does not mean "being away in a nice place." It refers merely to a respite from the everyday tasks that tire one and that one is tired of. When considered in these terms it is clear that being away is in itself insufficient to define a restorative experience.

Fascination derives not only from interesting things or places, but also from processes such as thinking, doing, and wondering. People are fascinated by figuring things out, by predicting, by recognizing. Such informational activities gain their fascination by the challenge of uncertainty or difficulty. Detective stories, stalking wildlife, and bird watching are all examples of such process-based fascination

Nature is well endowed with objects of fascination in flora, fauna, water, and the endless play of light. People also tend to be fascinated with natural processes such as growth, succession, predation, and even survival itself. 認知. 相容性

Compatibility. An environment may offer fascination and extent and still fall short as a setting for restorative experiences. The final property of restorative settings involves compatibility between one's inclinations and environmental circumstances. Such circumstances include both what the setting requires from the individual and what it offers in terms of information and opportunities. The compatibility concept is a bit more difficult to explain, but examples where such compatibility is missing may help to make the idea clearer. One might, for example, wish to relax and enjoy the sunset but feel called upon instead to watch for marauding mosquitoes. Or one might wish to walk in the woods but be expected to attend a family gathering. Alternatively, one might want to finish a project only to find that some crucial information is missing. In much of daily life the most striking information (the loudest, biggest, brightest, or most abundant) is not the information needed for action. These are all instances of incompatibility, and they add to mental fatigue.

Nature is a compatible setting for many human inclinations.

People often experience nature as particularly high in compatibility. There are many ways of relating to the natural environment that people seem to fall into rather readily. These include predation (hunting or fishing), domestication of the wild (gardening, caring for pets), and observation (bird watching, visiting zoos). Other activities that can be high in compatibility are closely related to survival, for example, fire building, constructing shelter, and even locomotion. People often choose natural areas with one or more of these purposes already in mind, so that compatibility is likely to be high.

Summary

Mental fatigue is a fact of life in a world overflowing with information. Finding ways to recover is greatly helped by the availability of restorative settings and experiences. Fortunately, it is possible to design and manage natural environments in ways that encourage recovery from mental fatigue.

Sharing Information

Design and management efforts depend on the exchange of information. The information exchange includes finding out about people's concerns as well as providing information to make their outdoor experiences satisfying. People require way-finding information to avoid getting lost, guidance to facilitate their understanding of a setting or restrictions to its use, and material that helps them anticipate the consequences of projected changes. Information exchange constitutes a major budgetary item for many agencies, not only for the production and distribution of printed material, but also for staff positions (such as public information officer) that are dedicated to garnering public support. Recognizing the importance of information exchange, however, provides little assurance of its success. The purpose of this section is to explore why sharing information often fails to be satisfying and to offer some suggestions for making such efforts more effective.

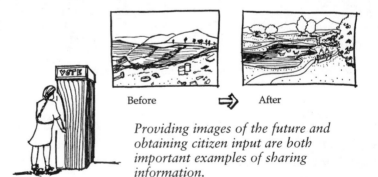

Before ⇨ After

Providing images of the future and obtaining citizen input are both important examples of sharing information.

Sharing information involves some interesting paradoxes. One of these is that despite their great desire for information, people often ignore information that is provided even if it is pertinent to their needs. What parent has not suffered the frustration of a child who is unwilling to hear sage advice? What adult has not turned a deaf ear to invaluable guidance? There is also a great disparity between providing information and receiving it. The human inclination to offer counsel is often not matched by the human inclination to receive it. Even when the information is requested, the recipient may fail to listen to the response. A classic example of this involves the discrepancy between the person who is offering richly detailed instructions for finding a particular destination and the person who had asked for the directions. The latter may have stopped listening after only the third landmark or turn in the route was mentioned. Discrepancies in efforts to exchange information often lead to inappropriate accusations that people don't really care as well as assertions about the stupidity or incompetence of the target person or group. These interpretations, however, reflect a misunderstanding of the failed efforts.

The child's game of "telephone" illustrates the difficulty of transferring information.

Building Maps in the Mind

Providing information is often straightforward, especially if one does not consider what is to happen to the information. However, the challenges of sharing information are all too often evident at the receiving end. Exchanging information requires transferring something from one head to another. Heads, however, are very different from other containers used for storing information. Unlike transfers between drawers, boxes, or files, such transfers cannot be accomplished by pouring, placing, shoveling, or dumping. Even *telling* does not necessarily lead to successful information transfer.

People carry many internal maps in their minds. Some of these correspond to places and store spatial facts, but mental maps are not limited to geographic information. They relate to events, activities, people, big issues, and trivial things. Such maps are the way that knowledge is stored in the head, and as such, we have maps for just about everything we know.

The process of exchanging information is closely linked to these maps. The maps were not placed in our heads by inserting floppy disks. The only maps each of us has are ones that we construct ourselves, and none sprout in an instant. They take not only time to develop, but a great deal of experience. Through many repetitions of similar circumstances, we construct these mental or cognitive maps. Information that did not recur in our experience is less likely to become part of the specific map. Contradictory information, especially if there had been few instances, is also likely to be excluded. These mental maps not only store our experiences in some organized fashion, they also are the basis for the way we receive information.

Being told something is not a sufficient basis for creating a map. If one already has a mental map that relates to what one is told, it is more likely that the information will be incorporated. By the same token, being told something that does not fit with our existing internal structures is likely to be met with resistance.

The Challenge of Information Exchange

The assumption that the recipient has internal maps that correspond to our own is probably the most basic of errors humans make in their efforts to exchange information. After all, each person's internal maps were individually crafted from unique experiences. To make matters more difficult, we have only a limited sense of how our experiences and stored knowledge—our maps—relate to those of another person. Awareness of these limitations makes it easier to appreciate how challenging successful information transfer can be. Here are some ways to make the process more likely to succeed despite the inherent difficulties. It is no accident that these considerations have in common that they focus on the targeted recipient of the information, rather than on the knowledge of the knowledge provider.

Is the information you're trying to teach people related to anything vaguely familiar?

Relation of information to what the individual already knows: This involves a delicate balancing act requiring consideration of three vectors: (1) People often resent being told what they already know, (2) They appreciate information that helps them expand on their previous knowledge, and (3) They often have trouble understanding and remembering information that is not connected to the maps they already have.

Dealing with information that may be upsetting: Here too there are interrelated issues that need to be taken into account: (1) People find negative information painful and will tend to avoid it, (2) They strongly dislike information that is confusing, and (3) They resist information that might undermine their world view.

Quantity and quality of information: (1) The most common and serious error in the presentation of information is to include too much. Even under the best of circumstances, when people are highly familiar with the material being presented and eager for it, their capacity for taking in new information is limited. For this reason people often find it easier to understand information if permitted to work with it at their own pace. (2) The flow of the information, for example, having a storyline or clear organization, also impacts the ease of transfer to the recipient's internal map. (3) Finally, the use of visual and spatial information in combination with words is far more effective than words alone. Both concreteness and having multiple examples help people understand and remember material.

Expertise and Local Knowledge

As we have seen, mental maps are the result of experiences gained in many ways. Much of one's experience is gained by virtue of where one lives, has lived, or has visited. Experience is also acquired from social patterns within one's culture, subculture, and family. Ethnic differences are a part of such experiences and so are the subcultural patterns of different age groups. Older people in this country have had vastly different experiences than did their grandparents; so too with adolescents. Still another major basis for experience comes from more systematic efforts, such as formal learning in childhood and throughout one's life.

Locals and tourists view the same area differently.

Despite the diversity of experiences in people's lives, the differences in their mental maps are generally invisible to them. Yet these differences, reflecting distinct perspectives or ways of seeing, are at the core of many tensions and conflicts. In the context of this book it is particularly important to mention the perspectives that differentiate experts from citizens. Of all the factors that lead to differences among groups, expertise is the one that has the greatest impact on the design, planning, and management of natural areas.

The process of becoming an expert involves acquiring a different way of seeing than one had before. In the early phases of learning, the budding expert might complain about all the new information and jargon of the particular field. However, as new mental maps develop, the memory of previous perspectives quickly fades and the expert is soon oblivious of changes. It is characteristic of experts to be unaware that their perception of a situation differs from the perceptions of those who do not share their expertise. A photographer sees the environment in terms of light; a park designer considers circulation patterns; a realtor is sensitive to property values. The same piece of land can be described in vastly different terms depending on these different ways of seeing.

Experts see the environment differently from one another.

The diverse ways of seeing are expressed not only in terms of different categories of information that are considered important, such as circulation or property value. They are also reflected in many subtleties and details that are part of the specialized understanding. Imagine two individuals, one a naturalist and the other a computer expert. The former might be awed by the diversity and beauty of a marsh, while the latter is bored by its sameness. By the same token, the latest version of an operating system might lead to rapture in the computer expert, while the naturalist may find it basically similar to any other such system and hardly worthy of notice.

The knowledge citizens have about their local community—both its people and plants—is also a form of expertise. Cognitive maps about available nearby natural settings and their use patterns are acquired in the same way as the internal maps of experts. This form of expertise also comes with a lack of realization that others do not share one's way of seeing.

Each of the perspectives represents the accumulation of experiences of its owner and thus constitutes the person's reality. While they are all appropriate and useful ways of seeing; no single one of them has exclusive "truth." Nonetheless, differences between professionals and local residents can lead to sharp disagreements and strong animosities. When things get sufficiently out of hand, there are mechanisms for getting the sides to hear each other and resolve the conflicts. There are also legal means of handling such situations. From our perspective, however, it is even more desirable to prevent some of these clashes from happening. Understanding the nature of internal maps and the limitations they place on information transfer can be helpful in integrating professional insights with local wisdom. We will return in the chapter on "Engaging People" to many of these topics, where we suggest some ways to incorporate local knowledge in the design and management of natural settings.

A local person may recognize subtle difference in hilliness amidst apparent flatness.

Summary

Most of our waking hours are devoted to the exchange of information: everything we say or write, read or watch on a screen is part of such an exchange. Some of these efforts work well; others are exercises in frustration. The challenges of sharing information require understanding the impact of experiences on mental maps; people's diverse experiences, in turn, affect their distinct perspectives. The pervasive differences between experts and the public are particularly important to appreciate in order to foster more satisfying exchanges in the design and management of natural settings.

Concluding Comments: Themes and Variations

In designing and managing nearby natural areas both commonalities and variations among people must be considered. The assumptions that people are basically similar and that one can rely on one's own experiences in designing and planning for others are likely to lead to unfortunate consequences. It is extremely difficult to appreciate how much our perceptions have gradually changed in the course of our experiences.

The various themes discussed in this chapter represent pervasive human characteristics. People care deeply about information. They dislike confusion; they love to explore. People's fatigued mental state is restored by activities that are fascinating and compatible with their purposes. All of us rely on the mental maps we create as we acquire information and experience.

Our mental maps, however, are vastly different. Our choice of what, when, and where to explore is varied. Our approaches to recovering our mental fatigue take many forms. Thus, much as the themes are universal, their resolutions or modes of expression are diverse. Such variations characterize the same person on different occasions or phases in life as well as different individuals depending on circumstances. Persons with mobility limitations desire opportunities for exploration as much as anyone else, but might go about such activities differently. First-time visitors to a park look to different cues in the setting to enhance their way-finding than repeat visitors. People with extensive ecological knowledge find disarray in patterns that those lacking such background cannot notice.

Thus in putting the material presented in this chapter to use it is important to consider both the themes and their variations. Basic to human well-being is an environment that fosters understanding and provides opportunities for exploration. Both of these needs, however, are changed with ones' experiences. Comparably, while psychological health is also improved by restorative opportunities, familiarity and experience influence what leads to the recovery of mental fatigue.

Much as people are eager to exchange information, sharing it involves far more than telling others what one knows or thinks. The love of telling others is often equaled by their resistance to being told. In the process of exchanging information one may discover that the perceptions one presumed to be pervasive are actually unshared.

Each of the themes introduced in this chapter will appear again in later chapters. They are central to the remainder of the book.

Part II

Meeting the Challenges

Chapter 2 explored some characteristics humans share. The environment can be helpful with respect to these characteristics, making it easier for people to function effectively. All too often, however, our environments fail to support human needs and inclinations. In some cases, incompatibility between people's needs and the environment is difficult to avoid. Examples include short-range inconveniences while changes are being made as well as long-lasting situations, such as a work environment without a window. Sometimes conflicting needs lead to a supportive setting for some but not for others. The costs of these and many other incompatibilities are often relatively invisible and readily ignored. We tell ourselves that people are adaptive, that they can grow accustomed to increased pressures and to less contact with nature. In the process, however, we as individuals and we as a culture are changed. There is evidence that under such conditions we become less sensitive to fellow humans. Perhaps we also become less connected to the natural world around us and less sensitive to environmental degradation.

In part II we offer some approaches to the design and management of the everyday natural environment that address these psychological costs. Chapter 3 focuses on *fears and preferences*. Fear is an important cost. Often the adaptive solution to dealing with a feared setting is simply to avoid it. Such decisions can have unfortunate consequences. Settings that are not used can be interpreted as not being needed, and that, in turn, might be used to justify their conversion to other uses (an example is the elimination of parks and open spaces in the urban context). Low use can also increase the likelihood of use for illicit purposes, leading to increased fears. Fortunately, some apprehensions can be addressed through design and management.

Preferred environments are important because of the ways they can enhance people's effectiveness. Preference, in our view, does not concern amenities or luxuries. Rather, preferred habitats for humans as well as other creatures are those settings that are supportive of mind and body. Designing and managing environments to enhance preference requires attention to the understanding-and-exploration ideas introduced earlier.

Chapter 4 concerns *way-finding*. Being lost can be uncomfortable and even terrifying, but one way to address the issue of way-finding is in the design of the setting. Way-finding is frequently handled by providing material to orient the user or visitor. Maps and signs can be helpful; often, though, they add to people's frustrations rather than reducing them. The second part of the way-finding chapter deals with ways to make maps more user friendly.

Chapter 5 discusses *restorative environments*, settings that are intended to offset the effects of mental fatigue. As we noted earlier, mental fatigue is a condition that is widely experienced and has the potential of seriously undermining human effectiveness. Creating and maintaining restorative settings thus has some urgency.

The three chapters of this part are organized in terms of the pattern concept described in chapter 1. The patterns given here draw on a great deal of information, including the research literature, insights from practitioners, and the conceptual framework that has guided the book as a whole. For the most part, however, these sources of information are not specifically mentioned in the material presented in the chapters. Sources are listed in "Readings" at the back of the book.

The presentation of patterns follows a common format. Each pattern has an identifying number. (F1, for example, is the first pattern in the "Fears" section, while P1 is the first pattern in the "Preferences" section.) Each pattern has a brief name, which is followed by a short descriptive statement. The text and graphics then develop the theme of the pattern. To repeat what we said earlier in the book: The intention of the patterns is to provide an approach not a prescription. These are not rules but recommendations. There is no such thing, in our book, as a unique solution that can be right for all times and all places.

Chapter 3

Fears and Preferences

Knowing what people prefer is important. People not only get more out of an experience in a place they prefer, they are also more likely to go there in the first place. But the downside of preference is also important to consider. Being in a setting that is not preferred can have unfortunate consequences. People may get bored or angry or even destructive. They also may be fearful.

One reason some places feel uncomfortable and others seem congenial is familiarity. Even if we have never been there before, a place may feel familiar by reminding us of another place we know. But familiarity is not the whole story. Some places that are novel are intriguing, and other places are all too familiar.

A feeling of fear or comfort can be produced by the physical layout of a setting. Places can be arranged so that they are easy to understand and will encourage exploration. When the needs of understanding and exploration are not met, people may feel frustrated and even threatened, adding to their fears and apprehension.

Without even realizing it, people quickly make decisions about places that translate to the feelings of fear or comfort. Those decisions are closely related to what they can see (visual access) and whether it would be easy to move through the area (locomotion). If that quick evaluation signals obstacles, the desire to go farther is reduced.

The ideas of visual access and locomotion, as well as the understanding-and-exploration framework, are the bases for many of the patterns presented in this chapter. We examine the topic of fears first and then turn to the topic of preference. These issues are closely related, however, and many of the patterns would fit under either heading.

The patterns:

Fears	*Preferences*
F1 *Visual access*	P1 *Coherent areas*
F2 *Enhancing familiarity*	P2 *Smooth ground*
F3 *Human sign*	P3 *Mystery*
	P4 *A sense of depth*
	P5 *Openings*

Fears

Some fears are appropriate. Many others, however, are based on a lack of familiarity. Regardless of their origins, fears are major obstacles. Fortunately, through proper design and management of natural settings the potential for fears in those areas can be reduced.

The patterns in this section address the following issues:

- The stated fear is not necessarily the underlying concern.
- Telling people that their fears are unwarranted is unlikely to be effective.
- Finding ways to increase visual access can reduce apprehensions.
- Creating confidence about way-finding (discussed in the next chapter) is an important component of managing fears.

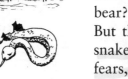
It is not at all unusual for children and even adults to express a fear of snakes and bears when they think about going to a natural area, even when it is in an urban setting. Do they really think they will meet a bear? Well, yes, in some ways they really think that. But their fear is of other things as well. Bears and snakes are a shorthand to express this collection of fears, many of which are difficult to articulate. They might include the fear of getting lost, of not knowing what information might be important, and of other unknown and unexpected possibilities. Many of the concerns and anticipations of discomfort have their basis in uncertainty, in a lack of understanding because of minimal experience.

Feeling safe is a prerequisite to the use of urban open spaces. There is by now an extensive literature on factors that increase people's sense of safety (see "Readings").

F1 Visual access

➤ VISUAL ACCESS INCREASES CONFIDENCE.

Blocked or obstructed views can create fear and concern. There are various ways that views can be blocked. Built components, such as low walls, can obstruct the view and provide hiding places. Vegetation can be so dense that it is impossible to size up the safety of a place.

The view would, of course, be least obstructed if there were nothing there, but that would hardly provide a reasonable solution to the problem of fear and the question of safety. It is more useful to think about ways to provide visual access without excluding or eliminating vegetation.

These scenes show the conversion of a blackberry thicket to a meadow. "The project opened up views into the site, improved recreation satisfaction (over 4 miles of trail), and dramatically increased the wildlife value of the site," according to Dan DeWald, the Natural Resource Manager for the City of Bellevue, Washington.

In designing or creating new areas, visual access entails the choice and placement of plantings. Settings such as apartment communities, visitor centers, and even public buildings feel safer if the arrangement of the plantings permits visual access so one can be aware of the behavior of others.

Trees with canopies and little obstruction at eye level make for settings that feel safe and also speak to what people prefer. However, not all trees are suitable for such treatment. Nor is it appropriate to follow such procedures in all places. Pruning low branches, for example, can allow more light into the forest floor and result in undesirable changes for flora and fauna. Underbrush may grow more rapidly, in time making for lower visual access and requiring greater maintenance.

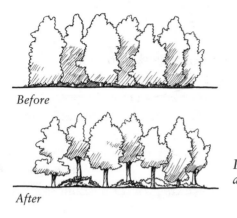

Before

After

Pruning dense vegetation at eye-level allows better visual access.

Keeping the view open and accessible may be especially important near paths. Dense vegetation next to a trail can be particularly problematic. In dense wooded trails, for example, removing tall shrubs from the immediate trail edge improves visibility and enhances the sense of safety. Longer views from paths and trails can also be provided by creating overlooks and by routing the path along ridges or higher areas. (See chapter 7, "Trails and Locomotion.")

Before	*After (1)*	*After (2)*
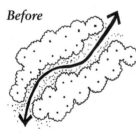	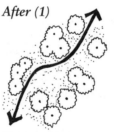	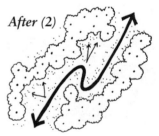
Plan	*Plan*	*Plan*

Sketch	*Sketch*	*Sketch*
Dense vegetation along a trail blocks views.	*Clearing vegetation opens views and increases the perception of safety.*	*In the case where external views are undesirable, internal views can increase visual access while retaining buffers.*

F2 Enhancing familiarity

➤ FAMILIARITY HELPS PEOPLE FEEL MORE COMFORTABLE.

When one is going to an unfamiliar metropolis that is reputed to be high in crime, others' reassurances that "it is really a safe place" often do not ring true. It is no different with snakes and bears. When one fears their presence, being told that such creatures have not been seen within a hundred miles is not always reassuring either. However, one can shed some of those fears as one gains experience and familiarity.

How can we encourage initial experiences despite such fears and concerns? Visual Access (pattern F1) certainly helps, so does being sure that finding one's way will not be a problem. It can also be useful to remind the individual of prior outings that proved enjoyable.

Taking small steps into unknown territory increases familiarity.

Familiarity is not gained instantaneously; it is the result of many small increments. Some such increments can be achieved by having a more experienced person lead the way. Short interpretive trails provide another means of enticing the visitor into an unfamiliar landscape. Having such trails within easy reach of parking and providing self-guiding brochures or posted material can also help.

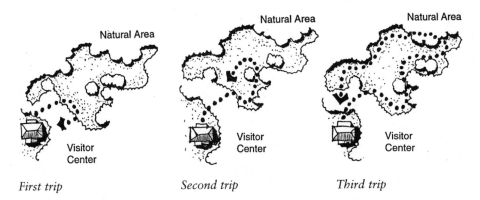

First trip   *Second trip*   *Third trip*

Enhancing familiarity means taking those first, timid steps into unfamiliar territory. Repeating the adventure is less risky and beckons one to venture farther.

The two photos below have been used in several studies. The photo on the left often produces considerable variability in preference. It is very much liked by residents for whom this is a familiar setting. For residents who lack such familiarity, however, the photo is often extremely low in preference. The trees are seen as "dead," the setting as "wild." The photo on the right, showing a tamer form of nature, is preferred whether or not it is a familiar setting. This is not to say that wilder nature should be avoided or that everyday nature must be tame. However, for many people, the tame and the familiar are essential if they are to be actively involved in the natural environment.

The "wild" nature (left scene) was frightening to many study participants who were unfamiliar with such settings. By contrast, the "tame" nature (right scene) feels safer to many people.

F3 Human sign

➤ Although indications of human presence can be a source of concern, human sign is often reassuring.

People are extremely sensitive to indications that fellow humans are present or have been in a setting before. Human elements in the natural setting are often comforting and highly preferred. At the same time, however, signs of human presence can signal threat or caution. Fences and barriers that mark a place as someone else's territory, for example, can lead one to be careful in one's exploration. Vandalism and other signs of destructive actions lead one to be vigilant and wary.

Human sign that makes one cautious.

There are many settings where the influence of human-made elements is positive. Nassauer (1995b) provides an insightful analysis of the perception of human intentions in people's appreciation of the landscape. Many people— farmers and rural residents, as well as suburbanites—express a preference for fields with a mowed edge. These, Nassauer argues, are expressions of hard work and pride, which help to communicate a sense of caring. Other indications of careful management of natural landscapes—such as pruning, cutting dead wood, or an abundance of flowers—have also received widespread acceptance.

Fences and walls can also be positive signs of human influence in natural areas.

The mown edge along a native grassland trail gives cues about human care (right) that are lacking in the scene on the left.

In many studies on people's environmental preferences, the scenes that receive the most favorable ratings are ones that include both a natural setting and clear human influence. The photos below provide examples from several studies carried out in diverse settings.

These scenes, from three different studies, each received the top preference rating. They reflect distinctive human influences. In each case, however, the human-made elements show a compatibility with the natural setting.

Preference: Enhancing Understanding and Exploration

Some nature settings provide a sense of comfort and serenity, invite one to wander freely with no concern for getting lost, and retain their charm even with many return visits. Many Japanese gardens offer excellent examples of such compelling and pleasurable places.

The patterns in this section address the following issues:

- People can very quickly discern how much they would like a place. Without realizing it, they seem to imagine themselves in the setting and rapidly assess how well they could function if they were there.

- Understanding and exploration involve decisions about the visual information—how easily one can see, how easily one could hide.

- Understanding and exploration also involve decisions about locomotion—how easily one can enter the setting and move about.

Considerable research on preferences for different kinds of environments shows strong consistencies (see "Readings"). It is hardly surprising that obstructions are disliked; they reduce both visual options and the sense that one could move through the area. It is also the case that wide open, undifferentiated areas are perceived to lack charm. In such instances, legibility is greatly reduced and complexity is lacking.

Research results, as mentioned earlier, also point to the important influence of mystery in increasing preference. To achieve such mystery one must have a partial view of things to come. When portions of the scene are partially hidden, one is compelled to seek, to find out about the rest. The charm of a foggy landscape reflects that characteristic. One cannot design fog, but there are plenty of other ways to introduce mystery into the landscape.

P1 *Coherent areas*

➤ A SMALL NUMBER OF COHERENT AREAS MAKES A SETTING EASIER
TO UNDERSTAND.

Consider a location that will become a roadside rest area. It is relatively
flat with some topography in one section that is not adjacent to the road.
The plan calls for minimal facilities but includes areas for walking, plus
five picnic tables and three grills. The budget permits a variety of trees,
shrubs, and ground cover. There are many ways that these "pieces"
(trees, shrubs, tables, grills) could be arranged. The solution can make
the difference between a coherent, intriguing, legible setting and one that
is not worth the stop. This pattern points to the importance of having
clearly identifiable areas or regions and not having too many of them.

*Hedges, fences, and ground covers create a small number of areas that
define this casual picnic spot.*

Areas achieve coherence by having similarity of plant species and/or
function and by being distinguishable from other areas. The borders or
edges between areas play an important role in helping the viewer understand the scene. Hedgerows, paths, fences, and texture changes can all
be helpful in designating areas.

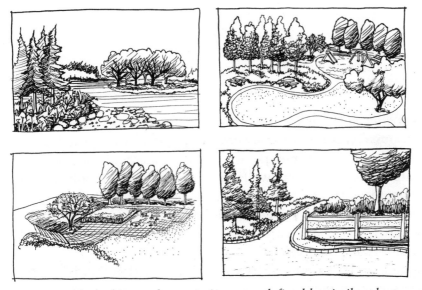

Some ways to achieve coherence: Areas are defined by similar plant material and/or functions, as shown in the top row. Texture changes can help define areas (bottom left). Borders between areas, such as paths and fences, further increase coherence and help viewers understand the scene (bottom right).

A large area can be divided into smaller areas with the addition of tree groves.

P2 Smooth ground

➤ GROUND TEXTURE IMPACTS PREFERENCE.

People experience the texture of their surroundings along each of the planes: ground, vertical, and overhead. Pattern F1 (Visual Access) focused on the vertical plane, pointing to the potentially negative influence created by impenetrable walls of vegetation or other obstructions. By contrast, the emphasis in this pattern is on the ground plane because of its special importance in permitting locomotion. The sense that one could readily traverse an area should one want to is a key component of feeling comfortable in a setting.

The texture of the ground also provides information that is helpful in understanding how the space is organized. Different regions, or areas, are likely to be marked by differences in the ground texture. Paths often have smoother textures than the adjacent ground, for example. This helps define regions; it also suggests that movement through the setting would be unimpaired. (See also chapter 7 "Trails and Locomotion.")

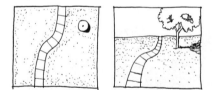

1. Too much smooth ground is monotonous.

2. Wide areas of smooth surfaces are more interesting when broken up with different textures and forms.

3. Being able to see more than one smooth area opens up the possibility of future exploration.

4. Smooth surfaces along trails add to the perceived width.

While it is possible to have too much of a good thing, in general smooth texture enhances preference by providing opportunities for locomotion.

P3 Mystery

➤ MYSTERY ENCOURAGES EXPLORATION.

Mystery, as used in the Preference Matrix in chapter 2, refers to the idea that the promise of more information is intriguing. But not just any additional information would qualify. For example, imagine walking in the woods and coming upon a high stone wall with a locked wooden gate. While suggesting wonderment and novelty, there is no promise of further information, as the gate is shut and one cannot peek in. Even a small crack in the gate, or a lower wall that permitted a glimpse of the world beyond, would greatly enhance the sense of mystery. In other words, a partial view or a suggestion of what might be ahead makes the situation far more compelling.

There are many ways to achieve such mystery. Foliage can hide and reveal. So can trees if spaced in a way that permits a view between them without allowing one to see all that lies ahead. The winding path is the hallmark of mystery in a landscape; it makes one want to find out what is around the bend. A hedgerow, or narrow tree screen, also suggests that there is additional information without giving it all away.

Mystery beckons one to explore further.

Mystery is also accentuated by fog and mist as well as the interplay between light and shadows. While such ephemeral qualities are not the stuff of design, they are helped, for example, by the spacing of trees and by selecting species that permit light to filter through the branches to the forest floor.

The winding road suggests mystery.

1.

2.

Adding layers of vegetation creates the hide-and-seek element of mystery.

3.

4.

Mystery can be additive (top row) or subtractive (bottom row).

One of the values of a mature forest is mystery.

P4 A sense of depth

➤ LAYERS AND LANDMARKS ENHANCE THE SENSE OF DEPTH.

Depth provides a third dimension. It is an important ingredient in both understanding and exploration. By informing the viewer that there is more to see, depth can provide an invitation to explore. The exploration, however, can raise concerns about legibility; the depth cues suggest that one can go farther, but will one be able to find one's way back?

The sense of depth can be increased by having definable "bands" across a landscape. A vista that offers an expansive view is likely to have such horizontal regions that help define layers in the scene. Topographic variation is often helpful for achieving such depth.

Two examples of layers in the landscape.

Landmarks or distinctive elements can also create depth. A church steeple has long been a cue for orienting from afar. Landmarks can also be regional in character—for example, a human settlement amid farmland, a mountain range above a valley floor, or a cluster of pines at a trailhead.

Distinctive landmarks help orientation.

P5 Openings

➤ OPENINGS IN THE WOODS ARE COMFORTING BOTH WHEN ONE IS IN THEM
AND WHEN ONE CAN LOOK INTO THEM.

Openings permit easy visual access and free locomotion of an area that
is more restricted. They create welcome respites as one walks through
the woods.

*Openings provide visual relief
along a trail.*

The following scenes show an even-aged stand of Douglas fir in a
small park in Bellevue, Washington. A thinning program, conducted to
improve forest health and increase wildlife habitat quality, improved
visual access (see pattern F1) and enjoyment for visitors at the same time.

*Judicious thinning of Douglas firs created an
opening in the forest that permits improved
visual access, thus enhancing both wildlife
viewing and the sense of safety for users.*

An opening is likely to offer mystery, suggesting without revealing all that will be apparent once one reaches it. This can be accentuated by the sunlight that can filter into an opening. In addition, an opening can increase legibility by serving as a landmark. Thus both understanding and exploration are enhanced by openings.

Openings can be appreciated from within and when seen from afar. As such they can aid in orientation as well as in enhancing a sense of mystery.

Forest openings can help to orient visitors. They can serve as landmarks when seen from a distance or along a trail.

Chapter 4

Way-finding

Being lost can be terrifying. Fears of getting lost can contribute to people's decision to avoid unfamiliar natural settings. By contrast, feeling reassured that one will be able to find one's way can increase the quality and potential benefits of nature experiences.

The patterns in this chapter address the following issues:

- Reassurance about way-finding needs to be communicated directly, in the way a facility or setting is designed.

- Visitors need an understanding of the spatial organization of the setting. They need to know the locations of likely destinations and what routes lead them there.

- Way-finding can be enhanced by portable maps, posted maps, and signs. If not done well, however, such efforts can contribute to the problem rather than the solution.

 When people feel oriented and confident that they can find their way around, their eagerness to explore an area is increased, and their general anxieties are lessened. Making it easy for visitors to acquire that knowledge will contribute significantly to the quality of their experiences in a natural setting. Kevin Lynch talked about the importance of way-finding many years ago in his book *The Image of the City*. Since then studies in a variety of contexts have shown the negative impacts of being lost or disoriented (see "Readings").

Developers of large and complex amusement parks are well aware of issues related both to the way the setting is designed and to the schematic presentations offered to visitors in the form of maps. There are some interesting tensions involved in both instances: a place needs to be rich enough to invite exploration but coherent enough that one can understand it. The possibilities for exploration need to be communicated without forgoing reassurance that the visit will be manageable.

The chapter is divided into patterns that focus on environmental design, on the one hand, and maps, on the other. Although way-finding concerns with respect to both these domains must address issues of simplicity and distinctiveness, they meet these requirements in different ways.

Way-finding: Design

Way-finding is made easier by having distinctive, differentiable elements. Such elements can be specific objects or places that serve as landmarks. They can also be regions, making it clear that one is in one zone or area as opposed to another. The distinctiveness of such elements, where they are placed, and the number of them are all key aspects of designing for way-finding. The first set of patterns in this chapter thus deals with such design issues.

Way-finding: Maps

The second set of patterns addresses ways to provide maps for visitors in a user-friendly fashion. All too often, maps end up confusing people rather than helping them find their way. Sometimes it is even difficult to find the map. A good map is important not only in making the visitor feel more oriented and comfortable, but also in enticing the visitor to explore.

The patterns:

Design	*Maps*
WF:D1 *Regions*	WF:M1 *Orientation for the new visitor*
WF:D2 *Landmarks*	WF:M2 *Mapping for the mind's eye*
WF:D3 *Paths and signs*	WF:M3 *Labels and symbols*
	WF:M4 *Which way is north?*
	WF:M5 *Check it out*

WF:D1 Regions

➤ Coherent regions are helpful in way-finding.

There are many ways to designate regions within a landscape or natural setting. Depending on one's knowledge and experience, one might define regions in terms of ecosystems, land use, relative distance from one's viewpoint (e.g., foreground or background), or any of numerous other methods. Even without particular expertise, however, people categorize a landscape in terms of areas that are perceived to be similar. For example, portions of a landscape that have a common texture are likely to be seen as belonging to the same region. Such categorization is not necessarily a conscious process, nor is it necessary to have names for the regions. Settings that readily permit categorization into regions have greater coherence. (Pattern P1, Coherent Areas, deals with a similar concept in a different context.) Such settings also facilitate way-finding.

In a natural area, regions might include a picnic grove, meadow, forest, and river's edge.

Distinct regions in a landscape can be natural or human-made.

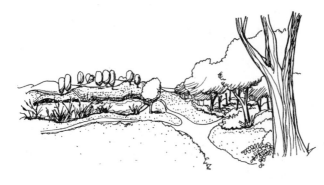

Identifiable regions help way-finding.

Regions offer a fast way to organize an area—both as one moves through them and when seen from a vantage point. If there are many regions, however, it is more difficult to remember them, thus reducing their usefulness for way-finding. There is no simple way to decide what makes for too many regions. Research findings would suggest that five is a reasonable number; seven distinct regions might tax memory. At the same time, having too few regions might also hamper way-finding. With sufficient experience, people might discern variation within a relatively homogeneous region, thus identifying meaningful subregions. For example, people come to discern different types of grasses within a prairie depending on minor differences in topography and moisture.

The scene on the left is an undifferentiated area, while the scene on the right is divided into distinct regions.

Too many regions (left scene) can make way-finding difficult. By contrast, about five distinct regions simplifies way-finding (right scene).

WF:D2 Landmarks

➤ LANDMARKS ARE MOST USEFUL IN WAY-FINDING WHEN THEY ARE DISTINCTIVE
AND NOT TOO MANY.

Landmarks need to be distinctive and memorable as well as visible from
some distance. They may be structures, such as a picnic shelter, or manufactured, such as an old-time farm implement. Natural features can also
serve as landmarks: a particular stand of trees, for example, a large fall-
en or hollowed tree or an opening in the forest. (See "Legibility" in chapter 2.) Nodes or major choice points in the path structure can also serve
as landmarks. Care must be taken that such intersections are not confusing, however; orienting signs may be needed as additional way-finding information.

*While nodes in a path system can serve as landmarks, a lack of orienting
signs may make them confusing. A landmark at a focal point along the
trail facilitates way-finding (right).*

*A fallen log can act as
a landmark along a trail.*

Old farm implements can act as useful landmarks.

As with regions too many landmarks can undermine their helpfulness. In order to help with orienting, the landmarks should be easy to distinguish. While it is important that the landmarks be distinctive, they should also be in tune with their surroundings. Distinctiveness that is jarring may not hurt way-finding but may detract from the overall experience.

Distinctive landmarks may help way-finding, but lack of harmony with the surrounding area can detract from the natural experience.

WF:D3 Paths and signs

➤ GETTING THERE AND BACK CAN BE AIDED BY PATHS AND SIGNS.

Way-finding is helped by coherence. If the viewer can easily oversee the landscape and understand the layout, it will be easier to remember. Violations of this notion are not hard to find in the built environment. Without signs directing one to exits, finding the way out of many a modern building can be quite scary.

In the natural environment paths that provide access to distinct regions and lead to landmarks are helpful to the novice visitor. It is also important to help the visitor distinguish between primary and secondary paths. Surface colors and textures, path widths, and adjacent plantings, are ways of enhancing the distinctiveness of different levels of paths. Such distinctiveness helps visitors become familiar with the basic structure of an area. While the concerns of the novice visitor are particularly important to consider, repeat visitors also benefit from paths that support understanding and exploration. (See chapter 7 on "Trails and Locomotion.")

Paths should provide access to distinct regions.

Primary and secondary paths can be distinguished by differences in texture, width, and adjacent plantings.

The path structure is also often communicated by signs and maps, which, as mentioned, have been known to create confusion rather than prevent it. This is an exception to the rule that every little bit helps—a poor sign or map is not better than doing without. Though well intended, such efforts might quickly confirm the visitor's suspicion that the setting is indeed too difficult to comprehend.

Since maps are frequently provided and often ignored, it is useful to consider approaches that would make them less difficult to read. The next chapter provides some themes to consider.

Path structure should relate to different uses and be communicated by simple, easy-to-read maps. (It is also important to remember that these materials will be read by individuals in wheelchairs as well as children.)

Symbols can sometimes be as effective as words for helping give direction.

As the illustration on the left suggests, simpler is often better for trail signage. By contrast, the trail sign on the right lacks clear definition of regions.

WF:M1 Orientation for the new visitor

➤ Key decision points need to be easily identified.

Maps can be used to provide an enormous amount of information. Much of the information, however, is unlikely to be helpful to the targeted user—in this case, a person unfamiliar with an area who wishes to explore it without getting lost. Such users are helped by having a map on which the visually strongest aspects provide an overview, emphasizing the main highlights and the path structure between them.

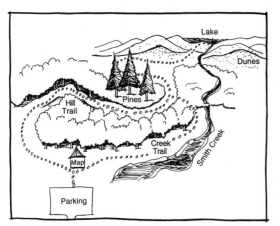

The intention of a good map is to support orientation rather than to replicate every detail of the environment.

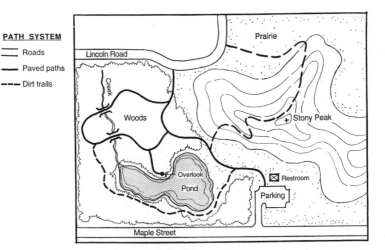

Maps should emphasize main highlights and path structure.

For those with great familiarity with an area (and for some mapmakers as well), it is tempting to provide more information than visitors can use, believing that people can simply ignore what they do not find helpful. Unfortunately, ignoring requires knowledge of the area that novice visitors are unlikely to have. The effect of too much information may discourage them from using the map at all and may even lead to the decision that the place represented by the map is too complex to explore.

The key is what to put in and what to leave out. A map designed as a legal document or one for road maintenance personnel needs to have different information than one that will help orient a novice visitor. It is, therefore, important to design a map in terms of its intended audience.

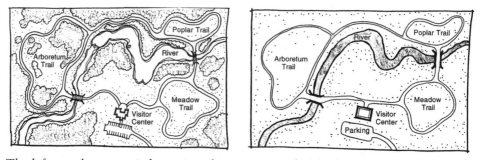

The left map has more information than necessary for the first-time visitor. The right map follows the "less is more" principle.

For the new visitor three categories of information need to be emphasized: (1) landmarks, the prominent and distinctive elements of the setting that anchor an individual's understanding it; (2) choice points, where a path branches and a decision must be made; and (3) large regions of relatively uniform content, such as "the woods" or "old farm."

Maps need to emphasize all of these categories of information.

The technique used for portraying different regions makes a difference in how easily the information is understood. Some maps, for example, use shading to show the intended area of the map and leave the surrounding area unshaded. The opposite approach might work more effectively, using only a light shading for the area beyond the site. This can make it easier to read the print in the target area. Shading everything to designate a distinctive region makes it more difficult to get an overview. Leaving portions of the map empty is often more helpful for communicating highlights.

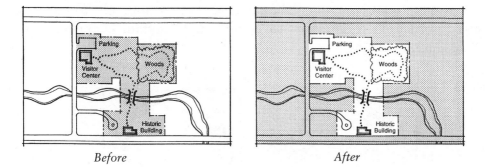

Before   *After*

Shading the area outside the map focus can make that area less dominant.

WF:M2 Mapping for the mind's eye

➤ AVOIDING THE ACCURACY HANG-UP LEADS TO A MORE EASILY
REMEMBERED MAP.

As we have seen in the previous pattern, a map is necessarily incomplete.
A good map cannot include all the information that is available nor
should it contain as much information as the mapmaker is tempted to
include. Perhaps even more counter-intuitive is the advice that a good
map not be totally accurate. The point here is certainly not to include
false information, but rather to communicate certain characteristics
while ignoring others.

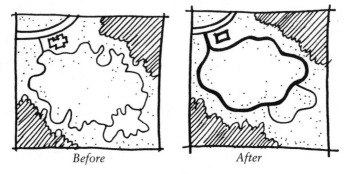

Before   *After*

*Showing every crook and bend in the path can be confusing
to first-time visitors. However, since a simplified map might
mislead the map user about the trail's length, providing
information about distance or time requirements is helpful.*

A common example of map inaccuracy is the way different kinds of
roadways are designated. The double red line frequently used to show
interstate highways does not reflect the actual width of the road. In fact,
depending on the scale of the map, a line of any width is not accurate.
Such exaggerations are not considered problematic because they are in
keeping with the purpose of the map.

In the same spirit, it is useful to consider other aspects of the map in
which exaggeration may be useful. Topography tends to be difficult to
communicate, and it can be helpful to accentuate elevation differences.
One could also consider it inaccurate if a map is not true to the undula-
tions in a path or river. From the perspective of providing the visitor with
useful orienting information, however, a somewhat straightened version
may be more effective.

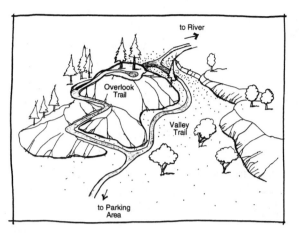

Exaggerated topography on maps can help way-finding.

A related issue is the angle of view taken in a map. A common practice is to use a plan view, which provides a straight-down perspective. This is particularly appropriate for showing the path or road structure. To communicate landmarks or noteworthy features in the environment, however, the plan view is less useful as it is hard to recognize these objects from a top-down viewpoint. By contrast, an oblique, or bird's-eye, view is easier to understand. The combination of a plan view for the paths and an oblique perspective for the landmarks yields a map that, while not literally accurate, is intuitive and reassuring. It permits the visitor to gain a quick grasp of both the layout and the placement of the featured attractions.

The rationale for permitting inaccuracies and using the more scene-like oblique perspective is to make the map visually meaningful and easy to understand. Such a map informs the user about what the setting is like, rather than presenting a replica of what is there.

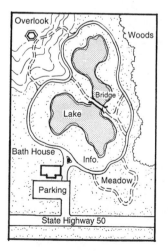

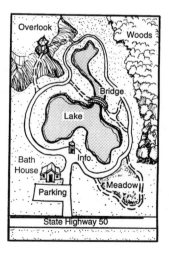

The plan of a map (at left) shows the path structure and major regions. The oblique perspective or bird's-eye view (at right) gives a better sense of the elements and their relationship to one another.

WF:M3 Labels and symbols

➤ MAPS ARE MORE HELPFUL IF THE INFORMATION IS WHERE ONE NEEDS IT.

People often find maps frustrating and confusing rather than friendly and enticing. Some of the problems stem from the placement of needed information. Comprehending a setting is more difficult when the user must go back and forth between the map and a legend. By the time one has found the key to the symbols and the translation of a particular symbol, one may well have lost the location on the map that started the search. An easy solution is to place labels right on the map, reducing the need for symbols. For example, replacing the symbol of a swimmer with the word "beach" at the same location on the map saves the map user the effort of looking up what the symbol means among all the others in the legend.

Symbols can be useful. It is important, however, that each symbol be easy to understand and that the list of symbols not be too long. Symbols are perhaps best used for recurring features or facilities rather than unique ones. If a particular symbol would be used only once on a map, it is likely that a label would be more user friendly. For example, a single sanitation station for trailers in a park could be marked as such rather than resorting to an icon that adds to the legend.

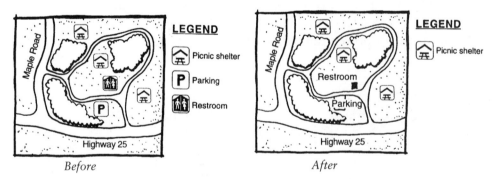

Before   *After*

Using symbols for features that occur only once can result in too many symbols. Instead, use symbols only for recurring features.

It is not uncommon for maps to include a numbered list of points of interest with corresponding numerals printed at the appropriate locations on the map, but here also the map would be easier to use if, instead

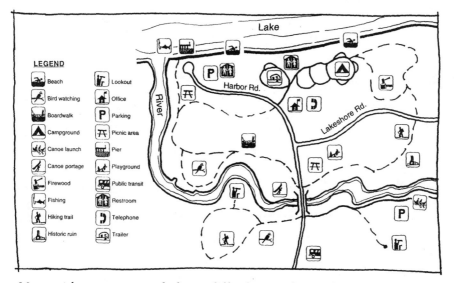

Maps with too many symbols are difficult to understand.

of the numerals, the points of interest were labeled directly on the map. Graphic representation of key landmarks can also be useful since they can be recognized immediately. The placement of the information—graphics and labels—right on the map makes the material more understandable and enhances interest in exploring the setting.

Easy-to-read maps have labels on important features.

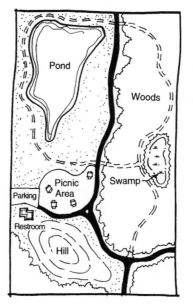

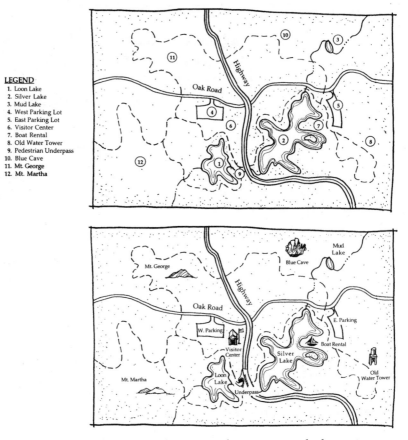

LEGEND
1. Loon Lake
2. Silver Lake
3. Mud Lake
4. West Parking Lot
5. East Parking Lot
6. Visitor Center
7. Boat Rental
8. Old Water Tower
9. Pedestrian Underpass
10. Blue Cave
11. Mt. George
12. Mt. Martha

Maps with a numbered list of "points of interest" might be easier to use with labels on the map and graphic representation where feasible.

WF:M4 Which way is north?

➤ ALIGN A POSTED MAP WITH THE VIEWER'S POSITION.

It is conventional to put north at the top of a map. With posted maps, however, that convention can lead to confusion for the visitor. A more useful procedure with fixed maps is to orient them in terms of the viewer's perspective, regardless of the cardinal direction. As the viewer faces the map, the bottom of the map should depict the area nearest the viewer, and the top of the map should depict what is farthest away. This approach would have prevented a frustrated visitor from carving into the wooden board on which a trail map was mounted: "This map is upside down."

Orient fixed maps to viewer's perspective regardless of the cardinal direction.

The bottom of a posted map should show the area nearest the viewer, while the top of the map shows the more distant views.

WF:M5 Check it out

➤ REACTIONS FROM POTENTIAL USERS CAN LEAD TO SURPRISING INSIGHTS.

The perspectives of the map designer and the map user are likely to be different. What may seem reasonable and appropriate to the mapmaker, may be confusing or overwhelming to a map user. Obtaining input from intended users can be very helpful for avoiding such problems.

Map designers can learn valuable insights from potential users.

A sample group could be asked to try out the map in draft form and to indicate what was helpful and what was burdensome. Was the amount of detail appropriate? Were they misled by anything? Did they feel comfortable with the map? Did it encourage them to explore the setting? Ideally, feedback would be sought from people who are not familiar with the mapped setting. They would be asked to try it out and to indicate what was helpful and what was burdensome in that context. (See also chapter 10, "Engaging People.")

Feedback from map users is vital to improve communication of way-finding information.

Chapter 5

Restorative Environments

R&R, or "rest and recuperation," is an acknowledged need for soldiers on the frontlines. It is not, however, uniquely the concern of the battle weary. Many people suffer from mental fatigue, decreased attention span, and irritability, and few seem to have an abundance of tranquillity, serenity, or peace of mind.

The patterns in this chapter address the following issues:

- Natural settings are particularly effective for R&R.

- They do not have to be dramatic.

- It is not essential that one is in the setting.

- Even a very short exposure can be helpful.

- Restorative benefits can be achieved even if that was not one's intention.

- One does not necessarily realize the gain immediately.

The importance of nature in restoration cannot be overemphasized. A natural setting can be small, quite large, or anywhere in between. The degree and kind of involvement with the setting can also vary widely, including hiking a nature trail, walking in an urban forest, planting or pruning trees, watching birds or squirrels, or simply viewing nature through a window.

A research literature on restorative environments is growing (see "Readings"). What may seem like a surprising finding (Hartig et al. 1991), that individuals returning from a wilderness trip are better at proofreading than members of a control group, serves as a demonstration of how restorative experiences can lead to a clearer head, making it easier to tackle tasks that require great concentration. Cimprich (1992) reported greater gains in recovering cancer patients who carried out nature activities (three times a week for about half an hour at a time) than in members of a comparison group. Tennessen and Cimprich (1995) showed that college students whose dorm rooms looked out onto natural settings performed better on attention-demanding tasks.

Restorative benefits are more likely to occur when one can feel secure enough to let down one's guard, when one can become absorbed in the environment without feeling vulnerable. (Patterns related to way-finding and reducing fear, discussed in previous chapters, also speak to issues that enhance restoration.) In the section on the psychological costs of managing information in chapter 2, we discussed several characteristics of restorative settings. Of these, extent and fascination are particularly amenable to design and management. They are, therefore, central to the patterns we propose in this chapter.

The patterns:

Restorative Environments

R1 *Quiet fascination*
R2 *Wandering in small spaces*
R3 *Separation from distraction*
R4 *Wood, stone, and old*
R5 *The view from the window*

R1 Quiet fascination

➤ NATURAL SETTINGS CAN FILL THE MIND AND ENHANCE RESTORATION.

Many things in the environment are fascinating. Fascinations, however, come in different forms. Some, let's call them "noisy"—such as spectator sports—tend to be distracting, making it difficult to think of anything else. What we are calling quiet fascinations do not totally dominate one's thoughts. They permit reflection; they make it possible to find out what is on one's mind. Many natural environments have the capacity to evoke quiet fascination.

Fishing, canoeing, and wildlife viewing are activities that involve quiet fascination. So is walking on newly fallen snow.

Quiet fascination can come from activities. For example, for some people activities such as gardening and fishing are mind filling. Quiet fascination can also come from the setting itself, from the sound patterns, the motion, the intensity of forms and color. The "action" in such a setting may be no more than the antics of birds and squirrels, the changing colors of the foliage. Fresh snow falling in the woods. The sun glistening on a drop of rain. Fancy coffee-table books filled with glorious photographs of everyday images of nature provide many examples of quiet fascination.

Open woods and rushing streams are just two of the many patterns of nature that can be fascinating.

There are many ways to provide for occasions that foster quiet fascination: places to stop and notice nature, for example, such as a bench at the water's edge or a footbridge permitting a view of the stream below. Even the view of a tree outside a window brings opportunities for observing its changes over the year's cycle and the chance to be engrossed by visiting birds.

A tree outside one's window can provide an opportunity to reflect on the change of seasons.

Footbridges are great places to observe nature.

R2 Wandering in small spaces

➤ EVEN A SMALL SPACE, IF IT HAS EXTENT, CAN CONSTITUTE A WHOLE DIFFERENT WORLD.

When people talk about getting away to a "whole different world," they are not referring to a setting that is different, but to being somewhere that constitutes a "world" of its own. What seems to be necessary to make a place a different world is extent, that is, the sense of extension in time and space. There needs to be the sense that there is more beyond what meets the eye, that one could go on and on.

A restorative environment permits the eye to focus on things that do not require any special effort yet are inviting and fascinating. In such a setting the mind wanders easily, absorbed by what the eyes take in, and also by one's thoughts. Such mental wandering is more likely when the setting gives the impression of having extent. While the *sense* of extent is important, the physical area need not be vast. In fact, vastness, if lacking in structure and interest, can interfere with restorative benefits.

Small natural areas around schools and workplaces can provide welcome restorative opportunities.

Depth and mystery in a small space.

The Japanese garden provides an excellent example of how extensive even a small area can seem. In addition to incorporating the ideas offered in the photograph below, such gardens pay careful attention to the details of nature (for example, stepping-stone pathways that compel one to stop and notice the small ferns or fallen leaves at one's feet). Other principles used in the design of Japanese gardens include open screens of fences or vegetation that divide larger spaces, circuitous pathways that create the sense of a larger area, and positioning viewing points so that the entirety of the garden cannot be seen from any one place. Many of these concepts are useful to consider in creating environments that are restorative.

Japanese gardens provide a sense of extent in a small place. The scene on the left is rich in mystery. In the scene on the right, the layering of interesting textures creates a sense of depth.

Put finer textures and darker colors in background.

Divide area into separate regions with layers of less densely foliaged plants.

Put bolder textures and lighter colors in foreground

Some ideas for creating a larger feel in a small space.

R3 Separation from distraction

➤ THE SENSE OF BEING IN A DIFFERENT WORLD IS EASILY UNDERMINED
BY INTRUSIONS AND DISTRACTIONS.

A place with extent is a coherent whole. It is free of interruptions and interference from things that do not belong. In the work setting, efforts to remove distraction often involve enclosure. Enclosures not only help focus on the immediate area and offer privacy, they also mark a separation from adjacent spaces.

Enclosures are also useful in removing distractions outdoors. A very small, "vest-pocket," urban park can effectively reduce nearby noise and distractions by creating a sense of enclosure. This can be achieved by using distinct textures underfoot and vertical features to mark its separateness, as well as by limiting the space overhead (for example, by a tree canopy). In larger natural areas the sense of enclosure can be realized by creating distinct "rooms." (See chapter 9, "Places and Their Elements.")

A small park can create a much needed oasis from busy downtown streets. A few canopy trees can provide separation from an urban environment as well as a restorative natural setting.

Restorative natural areas can even be created near industrial settings.

Separation from distraction can also be achieved in a large area that does not offer a sense of enclosure. Consider a setting that leads the eye to a distant place, a vista. In such settings, one is often unaware of much that lies between oneself and the vista because of its pull.

Courtyard plantings define a sheltered area while also providing restorative views from hospital rooms.

Enclosures can remove distractions. In addition, in certain settings, they can help focus attention on distant vistas and thus increase the perceived size of a small natural area.

Before

After

Enclosures can remove distractions.

R4 Wood, stone, and old

➤ THE CHOICE OF MATERIALS CAN ENHANCE RESTORATION.

Providing separation from distraction, marking a place as distinct, and permitting the mind to wander are all more likely to provide restorative benefits if the materials that are used do not themselves detract from the setting. The series of photographs here have in common that the materials that were used tend to be seen as fitting or appropriate to the setting.

Here a fallen log serves as a bridge for a wilderness trail (top) and as a rustic trail bench (bottom).

Fence material, the structure, stone steps, and wooden bench provide examples of materials that are compatible with their surroundings.

R5 The view from the window

➤ EVEN IF ONE IS NOT IN THE SETTING IT CAN HAVE RESTORATIVE BENEFITS.

Restorative settings come in many sizes, and restorative opportunities can vary substantially in length. A few weeks away from it all, in an appropriate setting should do wonders for one's R&R, but none of us can count on that to get from one day to the next. It is striking, however, that many of the benefits from restorative environments discussed here can be achieved by having a view from a window. Of course, to be restorative a view must have certain characteristics.

A tree outside the window can be mind filling. It tells about the seasons and the weather; it serves as the setting for diverse animal life; it symbolizes the past and promises a future. Even a single tree can make a difference. A view of a little grove of trees, a natural area, a garden, a pond . . . these all provide a context for the mind to wander, to take time out from pressing demands. Such views, indulged in even briefly, have been shown to affect health and well-being in many settings—home, work, hospital, and even prison (see "Readings").

A view from a window can provide the mental respite one needs to make it through the day.

The implications for design and management of natural spaces are vast and vital. A natural setting may be precious not only to its visible users, but to those who view it from elsewhere. The all-too-frequent occurrence of funds running out before "the landscaping" is done can have expensive repercussions in human costs. The landscaping is not just an adornment. If treated as the opportunity for increasing the sanity and welfare of those who can see it, it becomes every bit as important as hallways and lighting.

A view that allows the mind to wander.

A single tree outside the window can create a restorative focus.

A window that looks into the treetops can be especially engrossing.

Conference rooms can be greatly enhanced by adding windows.

Window views of ordinary nature can be just as satisfying as grand vistas.

Part III

Design and Management
Opportunities

In part II we discussed some of the psychological costs that arise when the environment is out of synch with people's needs. Environmental configurations that make it harder for people to be comfortable and effective occur all too frequently. The chapters in this part address ways to make those recurring problems less likely by considering contexts that arise in many natural settings. More specifically, these chapters focus on gateways, trails, views, relative size, and some specific landscape elements, such as trees and water. The patterns presented in this part of the book are not specific to particular land uses; they may be applicable in the design and management of parks of any size; in cities, towns, and rural areas; in residential areas, corporate sites, and many other settings.

The four chapters bring together many of the concerns raised in previous chapters. Earlier themes—understanding and exploration, restorative opportunities, and the complexities of differences among people—are still with us; they provide the basis for many of the patterns in this part. The importance of thinking in terms of people's interest in moving through a space (locomotion) and in seeing what is there (views) are also central to the patterns.

As in part II patterns are largely based on the research literature and, as such, do not cover all of the issues that must be considered in the process of planning, designing, and managing natural places. In other words, our purpose is not to be exhaustive but to highlight some human dimensions that are often ignored.

The environmental contexts addressed in this part are: gateways, trails, views, and places. *Gateways* are choice points; they signal a transition from one place to another. They provide opportunities for information about what lies ahead. The patterns presented in chapter 6 offer ways that gateways can help visitors to a natural setting with orientation and discovery.

Trails provide an important opportunity for locomotion. Making the experience of walking through a natural setting comfortable and interesting requires attention to the ground texture as well as to the path itself. While the intention of the trail is to accommodate movement, the view from the trail is also essential to the experience. The patterns presented in chapter 7, "Trails and Locomotion," address these points.

Much of our experience of nature is based on viewing it. Chapter 8, "Views and Vistas," explores ways to make such opportunities readily available and positive.

Chapter 9, "Places and Their Elements," highlights some environmental elements that have a significant influence on people's preferences. The patterns explore specific elements—trees and water—as well as some characteristics of spaces—their size and sense of enclosure. It is important to say once again that the patterns are not intended as prescriptions, nor can one offer fail-safe solutions that apply universally. While water is not always a delight, and trees are not invariably an asset, those features tend to play a vital role in the landscape. Similarly, there are no guidelines here as to what size makes a place "big" or "small"; nonetheless, issues of scale are important to consider when making design and management decisions.

Chapter 6

Gateways and Partitions

A partition is a fence, hedge, row of trees, or other form that divides an area. A gateway is an opening in the partition. It is a transition point, a place to pause and consider one's options. A gateway, whether natural or constructed, provides limited access to what lies ahead. Opportunities to look in are especially valuable. Since gateways depend on partitions, and since both enhance the experience of the landscape, we consider them together.

The patterns in this chapter address the following issues:

- Partitions and gateways help to orient visitors to an area. By subdividing an area, partitions create identifiable regions. They also define smaller settings, reducing the amount of environmental information that needs to be considered at any given time. Gateways enhance orientation by serving as landmarks and by providing a view into the next setting.

- Gateways signal a transition between "outside" and "inside." They provide views from outside that allow individuals to anticipate what they could experience within a setting. Even those who do not enter may enjoy looking in, and considering possibilities that they might take advantage of at another time.

- Gateways are choice points. They encourage people to pause and consider where they have been and where they may be going.

Both partitions and gateways meet many of the criteria for enhancing preference (discussed in chapter 2). Partitions provide punctuation to the landscape. This is a useful device for increasing legibility and adding interest to the landscape. Gateways also foster understanding and encourage exploration. The gateway can add coherence and distinctiveness, making it easier to make sense of

the natural setting. The limited access provided by the entryway is an effective way to increase mystery. The partial view invites one in and promises that more will be revealed as one ventures forth.

Gateways are not only effective in drawing one in, but they also encourage one to pause— to think, to choose, to remember. The development of a mental model of an area is facilitated by such moments, making way-finding more comfortable.

The patterns:

Gateways

G1 *Gateways need partitions*
G2 *Gateways and orientation*
G3 *The view through the gateway*

G1 Gateways need partitions

➤ PARTITIONS CREATE OPPORTUNITIES FOR GATEWAYS.

The first step is to consider ways to divide an area into separate regions; then access into a region can be provided through a gateway. Partitions include hedges, tree rows, wooded areas, and even hilly topography. The attraction of stone walls and split-rail fences might well be related to their usefulness in marking separate regions. As those examples indicate, the degree of separation can vary widely. A high stone wall may block vision and entry, except at the gateway. While an old, broken, split-rail fence may only suggest a separation, it may nonetheless be effective for defining distinct settings and for limiting access.

Partitions between regions can be rather open.

Plan   *Sketch*

hedges,

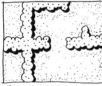

tree rows,

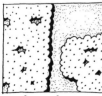

and woods.

Partitions come in many different forms.

Fences can define separate areas, yet still allow visual access.

The gap in a row of trees forms a gateway.

G2 Gateways and orientation

➤ A GATEWAY PROVIDES INFORMATION ABOUT WHAT LIES AHEAD.

The information provided by a gateway can suggest to a visitor some of the opportunities offered by the area, permitting an informed decision as to whether to enter, either now or at some later time. The gateway should also provide a sense of the general layout of the area, facilitating finding one's way. It is at the moment of pausing and deciding about entering that the visitor is particularly attentive to the general character of the setting. This makes the gateway an ideal place to provide an informative and representative view. The placement of the gateway can thus help the visitor become oriented to the setting ahead.

While signs are often used at gateways, they may be neither necessary nor helpful in orienting visitors. Sometimes signs are employed to counteract the problems created by poor design, but a gateway need not involve signage; its ability to aid in orientation can be intrinsic to the design of the entryway.

Information in the form of signage and visual cues occurs at gateways.

Gateways should give the visitor some idea of the opportunities offered by the area.

G3 *The view through the gateway*

➤ A WELL-DESIGNED GATEWAY CAN PROVIDE BOTH INFORMATION
AND MYSTERY.

While the partition may not afford any view, the gateway generally provides visual access into a setting. That view inward is enhanced by being limited, suggesting that more will be revealed as one proceeds. The view through a gateway is particularly effective if it offers a glimpse, or a suggestion, that encourages the visitor to imagine what will unfold as the next steps are taken.

Just a hint of a view encourages the visitor to enter a new space.

Exactly how to create the limited visual access, and how much to reveal at the entry, will vary with the context. The idea is to focus the view on elements that suggest what lies beyond. For example, at a trail-head, a canopy of low-branching trees can create a gateway that reveals only the base of a mountain and conceals the peak. In the same way, a gateway to a riverside trail may focus on an open woods and allow only a glimpse of the water.

The tree trunks and canopy form a gateway that provides a glimpse of the building associated with this garden.

Another way to limit visual access is to place the gateway off center from the main entry of a building or park and focus the view on some architectural clue such as a decorative fence, window, or roofline that hints at the function of the area beyond. (See "Mystery" in chapter 2.)

Limiting visual access helps create a sense of mystery through a gateway.

Chapter 7

Trails and Locomotion

Moving through natural areas is one of the most restorative of activities. Trails provide an excellent way to achieve this. The trails we discuss here are walkways within a natural area. Some of these are long corridors or trail networks; others are short paths through nearby nature. Our discussion is not about roadways or routes for motorized vehicles such as cars or snowmobiles, but rather emphasizes trails for walking, hiking, biking, skiing, and horseback riding.

The patterns in this chapter address the following issues:

- Trails through natural areas bring individuals into intimate contact with nature, allowing both observation and exploration.

- Trails invite one to proceed, thus enhancing a sense of security. In a setting that lacks trails it may be less clear that venturing forth is appropriate.

- Even people who feel guilty taking the time to enjoy nature may enjoy trails through natural settings while walking or biking to work.

A variety of studies have documented people's desire for opportunities to get away from all the unnatural things of city life, to enjoy natural beauty. The various activities that involve locomotion through natural areas provide popular means to fulfill such desires. Research based on photographs and slides has shown that people prefer that trails be compatible with the natural surroundings. This is evident in the ground textures people prefer, in the preference for paths that provide intimate contact with nature, and in the appreciation for trails that provide access to larger nature areas.

The patterns:

Trails

T1 *Trails, narrow and curving*
T2 *Views, large and small*
T3 *The trail surface*
T4 *The trail's path*
T5 *Points of interest*

T1 Trails, narrow and curving

➤ THE PROMISE OF DISCOVERING WHAT LIES JUST BEYOND THE BEND
IN THE ROAD GREATLY INCREASES PREFERENCE.

Many studies have shown that people are more attracted to a path that curves than to one that is straight; a sense of mystery is particularly important in the design of trails. The curving path should not be an arbitrary feature, however. The bend should follow the lay of the land or the pull of interesting landmarks. Mystery is particularly enhanced if there are strong hints about what will be seen as one proceeds.

Trails should curve to follow the lay of the land.

The width of the trail affects the intimacy of the experience. A trail that looks like a highway is convenient for maintenance vehicles; but that is generally at the expense of experiencing the natural setting. Neuropsychological research has shown that things within arm's reach are processed in a different area of the brain than more distant things. Thus it is hardly surprising that a wide trail that puts one physically more distant from nature increases the psychological distance as well.

The width of the trail influences the sense of intimacy with nature.

Although people like trails along the water's edge, in this example, the wide paved trail can significantly impact this fragile habitat.

T2 Views, large and small

➤ WHAT CAN BE SEEN FROM THE TRAIL MAKES ALL THE DIFFERENCE.

Trails that go through open areas with few trees or distinct features are less preferred. Trails through extremely dense woods or brush, affording little view, do not fare well either. In other words, each of the information factors that comprise the Preference Matrix in chapter 2 apply here.

Trails can be . . .

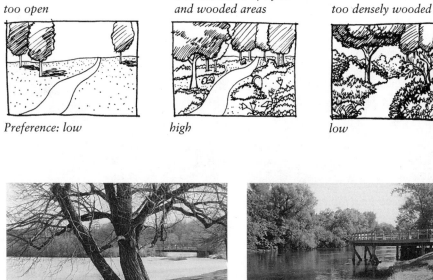

too open

a combination of open and wooded areas

too densely wooded

Preference: low   *high*   *low*

People appreciate trails near water. Viewing areas and trail location can help minimize the impacts.

While people appreciate trails that are near the water's edge and that provide a close look at plants, the vulnerability of the ecosystem must also be considered. Constructing viewing stations and lookout points is a way to minimize impact while permitting some contact.

T3 The trail surface

➤ Trail surfaces are important, both visually and functionally.

Trails with relatively soft surfaces are generally preferred, although asphalt or concrete may be more suitable for certain activities. Boardwalks in natural settings received high preferences in several photo-questionnaire studies. Boardwalks can be a good approach for permitting access to fragile areas, such as wetlands, that people would not normally see. Boardwalks also make it possible for people to pass through areas of dense vegetation without feeling uncomfortable.

Boardwalks can provide access to fragile areas with a minimum amount of damage.

The intended use of the trail is necessarily important in the choice of surface material. Nonetheless, the options may be greater than is often considered. Chapter 10, "Engaging People," shows some ways in which citizen input can be useful in making such decisions.

These are examples of trail surfaces that are well suited to walking or hiking. Top row: packed dirt and stepping stones; bottom row: gravel and wood chip.

T4 The trail's path

➤ HELPING PEOPLE STAY ORIENTED IS AN IMPORTANT FUNCTION OF A TRAIL.

The layout of a trail affects people's decision to use it. The design of a trail needs to facilitate way-finding. This can be accomplished by incorporating design elements such as visible access points and landmarks, which at the same time can make the experience more interesting.

Landmarks and bridges along trails help people stay oriented.

An interconnected system of trails, as opposed to a simple loop trail, can have great charm and attraction. However, if the user fears getting lost, the charm is greatly reduced and use of the trail may be decreased. The maps commonly posted at the trailhead offer little reassurance as the information they provide often exceeds the visitor's memory. The complexity of these trails thus requires careful attention to printed maps as well as signs at critical junctures to guide the visitor. (See chapter 4, "Way-finding.")

Some confusion can also be avoided by using different trail widths or surfaces to help with orientation.

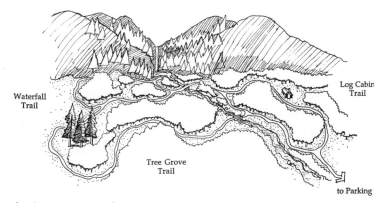

An interconnected systems of trails is more interesting to the visitor but also requires a map that is useful.

Landmarks along a trail, such as a waterfall, can help way-finding.

Signage can often help orientation, but also can detract from the experience.

T5 Points of interest

➤ STOPPING POINTS ALONG THE WAY CAN PROVIDE OPPORTUNITIES FOR RESTING AND OBSERVING.

Trails are more than routes; they provide opportunities. A trail that is relatively narrow and curving, with a pleasant surface and clear signs, may nonetheless fail to attract visitors. Trails that provide access to interesting view points and important features are particularly valued. Stopping points can serve as landmarks, as destinations, and as places to slow down and notice what is nearby.

A tree grove can be a landmark along a trail.

Benches along trails are welcome for resting. Not infrequently, while sitting and doing nothing, people notice the vegetation, the birds, the squirrels, the cloud patterns, even the topography. While one is moving along the trail, much of the surrounding world is background, but when one stops for a while and sits on a bench, the background becomes the focus.

Benches along the trail are important for both resting and observing nature.

Landmarks, whether built or natural, also offer occasions to stop and notice. Historical features, such as old farm equipment or remnants of buildings from the past, often provide an interesting stopping point. Huge trees, uprooted trees, hollowed trees, and many other natural features are also places where people are likely to stop and observe.

People appreciate the opportunity to see historical as well as natural landmarks. These can serve as destination points, providing a clearer purpose for the outing, or they can be features along the path.

Chapter 8

Views and Vistas

A great deal of our contact with nature is from a distance. Views and vistas are, by definition, enjoyed from afar. Even though one is not a part of the landscape one is viewing, one can get a great deal of satisfaction and other benefits from views and vistas.

The patterns in this chapter address the following issues:

- The benefits of a nature view are far greater than is generally realized.

- To say that views are enjoyed passively is to miss the point of their value. The active component comes not from locomotion but from cognitive involvement, from engaging the mind.

- Vistas provide a big picture, revealing the extent of what is out there.

- At the same time, vistas also provide a miniature in supplying an overview that makes it possible to put the pieces together.

Views and vistas are a precious resource. There is by now considerable documentation that providing a view, and especially one that includes vegetation, has positive implications for health and well-being. The importance of the view has been shown in studies of prisons (Moore 1981, West 1986), hospitals (Ulrich 1984, Verderber 1982), apartment residences (R. Kaplan 1985a), and the workplace (R. Kaplan 1993b). In the office setting, for example, those with views of nature felt less frustrated and more patient, found their job more challenging, expressed greater enthusiasm for their job, and reported higher life satisfaction and overall health.

It is striking how many of the themes that have been discussed previously are central to the topic of views and vistas. Views, as mentioned earlier, can play an important role in way-finding. In offering a bird's-eye view of an entire area, a vista can make it easier to develop a mental map of the setting. Even when the view is limited, information about what lies ahead can be helpful for orientation.

Consideration of what makes particular views or vistas enjoyable is closely related to the Preference Matrix (in chapter 2). Views enhance understanding and inform exploration. Even when the vista is far distant and one may never have a chance to visit the area viewed, it can offer the opportunity for a mental exploration. To appreciate the ways the Preference Matrix relates to views, consider a view that is blocked (a nonview). When the view is obstructed, one cannot tell what might lie ahead (mystery), whether there is a richness of things to see (complexity), or whether one could make one's way in the setting (legibility).

The idea of extent, so central to mental restoration, also applies to views. Looking out to a distant scene can offer fascination and the opportunity to let the mind wander.

In some cases, a setting can be designed both as a place for direct experience and as a place that can be viewed from elsewhere. Usually, however, design or management of vistas or views is not possible because they cover too large an area, are too distant, or are inaccessible for other reasons. The intention of this chapter is to promote making views and vistas available.

The patterns:

Views and Vistas

VV1 *Enough to look at*
VV2 *Guiding the eye*
VV3 *More than meets the eye*
VV4 *Think view*

VV1 *Enough to look at*

➤ A VISTA IS MORE ENGROSSING IF IT HAS EXTENT.

Consider a view out the window onto a large mowed area. Even if it is well maintained, such a green expanse is unlikely to be a favored view. The addition of a few trees can quickly enhance its quality, however. The trees not only provide interest in their own right, they also give the scene greater depth. Extent is increased by the expanded sense of depth and by the greater richness of elements in the viewshed.

A view of a large mowed area is unlikely to be a favored view. Trees, by contrast, contribute points of interest and form.

Condominiums with a view of a golf course have become quite fashionable. Many people who pay for such a view do not use the facility. Golf courses have extent; they often have variation in topography, in vegetation, and in the sense of depth provided by the balance between trees and open areas.

Buffer plantings along expressways can contribute a sense of extent when viewed from nearby apartment units.

Apartment complexes in the areas near expressways—once the edge of town—also often provide views that have extent. The area between the expressway and the apartment property is often left undeveloped, with a variety of trees, shrubs, and tall grasses. Such views are different from those of the manicured golf courses and may be even richer in the diversity of plants to observe.

When the richness of vegetation reaches a very high level, other considerations must be kept in mind if it is to retain its attractiveness. While some density of vegetation may be desirable for screening, visual access, sense of depth, and coherence of the landscape must also be considered.

Layered plantings of the same species can provide a sense of depth, and hence extent, while still allowing visual access.

VV2 *Guiding the eye*

➤ A CAPTIVATING VIEW PROVIDES INFORMATION ABOUT WHERE TO LOOK.

You are driving along and a sign announces, "Overlook 500 feet." It's time for a stop, the parking is convenient, and it's a lovely, clear day; you pull over in anticipation of a beautiful view. As it turns out, alas, you are disappointed. Some views are hardly worth the stop. Even if there is "enough to look at" (VV1) and the content of the view is not negative (e.g., a dump site), the vista may not be exciting.

For a vista to be engaging, it must have both coherence and focus. Distinct regions or groupings help organize the view and make it coherent. If there are too many groupings, it is difficult to decide what to look at. A grouping or region might be devoted to a particular land use (e.g., a farm, a settlement) or consist of a particular land cover (e.g., a forested area). It might also be a variation in the visual pattern within a particular land use or land cover, such as those made by different crops on a farm.

Regions can be made by patterns such as those of different crops in a farm field (left) or wetlands with distinct areas of water, wetland plants, and woods (right).

A focus is something contrasting that captures the viewer's attention. An entire region—for example, a village in a valley—might provide such a focus. Or it might be a distinctive building, such as a church on a hilltop. Sometimes such highlights take advantage of ephemeral conditions, such as the angle of the sun. In any event, the focus stands out as a starting point for examining a scene.

Both the focal point and the distinct regions serve as guides for looking. They help direct one's attention. An additional quality that can make a vista more engaging involves features that guide the eye from one area to another. For example, a row of trees between two regions is likely to fulfill that function.

The focus of this view is the distant downtown skyline. Tree plantings, which screen nearby homes, help to simplify this scene.

Sometimes a human-built element provides a focus by contrasting with a predominantly natural landscape.

Rows of trees between regions can guide the eye.

Paths and pond edging guide the view into this landscape. Plantings of similar evergreen trees around the pond also help to unify the scene.

VV3 More than meets the eye

➤ A VISTA ENGAGES THE IMAGINATION.

The top of the Empire State Building, the revolving restaurant in the Space Needle, the children's game "King of the Mountain"—these all provide views that are out of the ordinary. Many other view points also afford a bigger picture, a way to see more at once. Even viewing a park below from the balcony of a nearby tall building can produce a sense of wonder.

People are intrigued by the miniature. One of the delights of model train settings is that the reduced size of the components of the landscape makes it possible to see more of it at one time. By seeing more of the surrounding area at once, one can understand the landscape more easily. As the vista holds the viewer's attention, it permits the viewer to imagine wandering in the space and encourages a mental exploration of areas hidden from view.

A sense of the miniature can be created by views down from high points (left scene) and up to high points (right scene).

Looking down on a courtyard from a high-rise building provides a new perspective on the landscape.

VV4 Think view

➤ CONSIDER OPPORTUNITIES FOR PROVIDING VIEWS.

Peepholes in solid fences at construction sites are notoriously popular. The chance to see in a limited, partial way is characteristic of many settings that are high in mystery.

There are many windowless places. Schools have been designed with no windows in the classrooms, supposedly to reduce distractions. Many conference rooms, similarly, offer little chance to be connected to the outside world. Prisoners, hospital patients, workers in many industrial settings, and thousands of office workers also spend many hours lacking visual contact with the world beyond the walls.

Peepholes and other small openings allow views into areas that might normally be blocked.

Recognition of the importance of views has spawned a variety of creative products that are substitutes for the real thing, such as large pictures designed to look like windows with a backlit view of engrossing (and changeable) scenery, or images that bring a changing world to the individual whose only view is on the computer screen. Whether such ersatz views provide some of the benefits of the real thing remains to be established.

Scenic overlooks are one way to provide windows toward landscaped areas.

Courtyards can focus views to nearby nature.

Windows are, of course, a common way to increase opportunities for views. Nature centers provide an interesting example of settings where taking advantage of a view can usefully augment their purpose. Such centers have often been designed to enhance display space, permitting little connection between the site and the building interior. In quite a few places, however, such centers have incorporated a view out, made more comfortable by a seating area, for visitors to appreciate the birds and wildlife beyond.

There are also situations when, in the context of designing a particular setting, it is feasible to consider the view afforded from outside the setting. Designing the setting with respect to views from other vantage points is an important priority given the significance of the view from the window.

Opportunities for views are not, however, restricted to windows. There are many situations where providing a view should have high priority in designing a facility. Previous patterns pointed to the way in which a gateway provides a view (G3); trails as well can be made more interesting by the views they permit (T2). Grand views from scenic overlooks and more intimate views into courtyards also enhance people's experience.

Views from indoors can be enhanced by orienting windows toward landscaped areas.

This nature center incorporates a glass wall for wildlife viewing. A hawk silhouette sticker helps prevent birds from flying in the glass.

Allow views of woods between buildings.

Cluster windows around landscaped courtyards.

Screen parking so visitors view natural areas instead of a sea of cars.

Some ideas for creating views.

Chapter 9

Places and Their Elements

Places are given form and distinction by their elements and the way those elements are arranged. Our focus here is on such natural elements as trees, shrubs, flowers, lawn, and water, as well as human-made elements like benches, buildings, and footbridges. A place is defined by more than its elements, however. For example, two forests with the same numbers and species of trees, even if they are of the same age and are similar in their canopies, can nonetheless feel completely different. The spaces that are created by the location of the elements are critical in making places that work.

The patterns in this chapter address the following issues:

- People become readily attached to places.

- People assume a sense of ownership of places that, strictly speaking, do not belong to them.

- People seek places for solitude.

- Even highly familiar places can afford exploration.

 Water is an element of many preferred places, but water settings can also fail to please. The water's edge pattern (PE2) deals with ways to make water settings highly favored, while also considering the fragility of this resource. Less often acknowledged as a singularly important component of preferred environments are trees. Although many kinds of vegetation can contribute to appreciated places, the presence of trees has repeatedly been found to be of particular significance (PE1).

Even if they contain trees, however, all natural settings are not equally preferred. For example, a row of trees can create a dense, impenetrable mass or an intriguing screen.

Or the same trees, appropriately arranged, can define a protected and intimate area. Many preferred places provide such a sense of enclosure (PE5).

Secret gardens and cherished nature places come in many sizes and shapes. They are endearing; something about them is special. What makes them special? Why the fondness and possessiveness about certain places? It would appear that the reason lies both in the elements and their arrangement.

The patterns:

Places and Their Elements

PE1 *Trees*
PE2 *The water's edge*
PE3 *Big spaces*
PE4 *Small spaces*
PE5 *A sense of enclosure*

PE1 Trees

➤ Trees help make special places.

A single tree can make a big difference. This may be true in the view from a window, in a landscaped setting, or in a place for a lunch break. It can be engaging as it reflects changes in season or as a perch for a songbird.

Two trees near each other have the added advantage that they create a space. Consider the opportunities two trees can provide for squirrel chases, or the special spot created when one sits between them.

Research on people's environmental preferences points to the pivotal role that trees play. Scenes that are most preferred consistently include trees, and scenes with large trees typically receive high ratings. Further, the presence of trees has been found to relate strongly to residential satisfaction. While other forms of vegetation are also greatly appreciated, the fondness people express for trees is particularly noteworthy.

Trees have characteristics that create special natural places and can harken back to childhood memories.

Nonetheless, trees are not always favored; their placement, selection, and maintenance must also be considered. Dense foliage and dark settings are often low in preference. Even a single tree that crowds out the light may be undesirable. The preference for large and old trees, however, suggests the importance of preservation as well as the choice of tree species that are long-lived.

While empirical studies have provided considerable evidence for the particular role that trees and other forms of vegetation play, the reasons for the strong preferences can only be surmised. Trees provide shade and shelter; they impart a sense of permanence; they serve as landmarks to give the landscape form. Trees also offer numerous other benefits (e.g., reducing pollution, increasing energy efficiency). Recognition of the multifaceted benefits that trees provide is expressed by the vast increase in municipal tree ordinances that encourage much greater attention to trees in the urban context. That increase is by no means trivial, given the numerous situations where trees are few and far between.

Trees, in numbers and groups, define spaces. As these illustrations suggest, they also reflect the change in seasons.

Community tree-planting projects have become popular in many cities, providing opportunities for citizens to be involved not only in the planting, but also in stewardship to make sure that the trees survive. Such programs have produced many associated benefits in the forms of community spirit, job training, and personal growth. It is impressive how much they yield for a modest investment.

PE2 The water's edge

➤ THE TREATMENT OF THE WATER'S EDGE IMPACTS HOW THE WATER IS PERCEIVED.

There is no denying the attraction of water in the landscape. Property adjacent to water—whether a pond, lake, stream, river, or ocean—is often more expensive. In recent decades many cities have invested in waterfront revitalization projects to make such areas strong commercial attractions. In many places waterfront areas have also been developed as greenways, providing opportunities for walking and biking as well as observing nature.

It would be misleading, however, to think that the presence of water assures pleasant scenery. Characteristics of polluted water (e.g., its smell and color) and the sight of foreign objects in the water can quickly detract from an otherwise scenic setting. Some of the plants that do belong, although essential to the habitat, might also contribute to an unkempt appearance.

Of particular importance in how water is perceived is the water's edge. A waterway that overflows its edge can look less attractive. And while unkempt or eroded edges have resulted in lower preference ratings, hard-surface solutions for containing the water can also generate unfavorable public reactions.

Waterscapes that are particularly appreciated tend to have edges that follow a more natural form, rather than being bound by straight edges. The presence of vegetation at the edge also can enhance the appearance.

The water's edge has a strong attraction and provides a popular location for greenways.

Vegetation along the water's edge often contributes to people's appreciation. Ponds with natural forms tend to be preferred.

Water is not always a guarantee of pleasant scenery. Eroded and overgrown banks, as well as flooded streams are generally disliked.

Straight, hard-edged solutions to erosion problems are also generally disliked.

PE3 Big spaces

➤ BIG AREAS BECOME MORE INTERESTING IF DIVIDED.

Though a vast view can be engaging, being in a big outdoor space can be quite daunting. In fact, humans as well as other animals are discomforted by crossing big, open areas, preferring to stay near the edges. Large areas also can be challenging in terms of the amount of information one may have to keep track of and may create difficulties in wayfinding. Dividing a very large area creates distinctive regions and therefore a safer, more manageable setting.

People are often intimidated by large, open spaces. Around housing complexes, such large undifferentiated areas can be problematic because they are not perceived to be "owned" by the residents.

Vast open areas can also make it difficult to know who belongs and who is intruding. The notion of "defensible space" (Newman 1972, 1995) arose in the context of public housing, where many areas were not clearly defined and a sense of safety was limited to one's own private unit. Newman showed that many of the notorious difficulties of such housing can be averted by creating distinctive areas that are semipublic, whose "ownership" residents share. When residents are jointly responsible for their turf, it is clearer to potential intruders that their presence would be noticed. Such feelings of shared ownership can apply to the space around apartment buildings, and even to the area around a picnic table in a park. Thus, the idea of defensible space extends beyond the urban residential context to other settings as well. Neighborhood parks, community gardens, and other situations where ownership is by a group rather than by individuals, and is conceptual rather than legal, are helped by design and management approaches that distinguish semipublic from public spaces.

A few trees can go a long way toward making a large space inviting. Similarly, landscapes divided into regions are more interesting.

Large mowed areas, whether around corporate campuses, within residential complexes, or in recreation areas, often seem uninviting. The Preference Matrix in chapter 2 suggests some concepts for designing such areas that might yield better results. Rather than endless lawn, a few differentiated regions, as well as some distinctive highlights, increase legibility. Providing a sense of mystery—for example, through topographic variation, winding paths, or the partially obscured view created by an open forest—would make a large area more interesting. Large areas also benefit from designing places that afford a sense of enclosure (see PE5).

A corporate landscape does not have to be faceless, as shown on the right.

PE4 Small spaces

➤ To be highly prized, places need not be large.

Some small places are very much appreciated. People savor memories of childhood tree houses. Many other hideaways are also not distinguished by great size. Even a window box can serve some of the qualities of small spaces.

Small spaces are not attractive simply because they are small, however. For example, research has shown that residents of an apartment complex strongly disliked their very small front yards, which were intended as a trade-off to permit larger common spaces. The front yard area was not large enough for residents to mark their territory, to use, or to make attractive.

A window box can help create a prized small space.

Enclosure and attention to detail can create inviting small spaces.

Even modest opportunities for personalization are appreciated by residents.

These spaces were perceived by residents as too small to be attractive.

What many effective small spaces have in common is that they impart a sense of extent despite their size. As we saw in "Restorative Environments" in chapter 5, despite limited physical dimensions, settings can permit one to explore. One can wander, for example, in a small city park, forgetting how near it is to major roadways. Interesting features, easy-to-follow trails, and sufficient tree cover allow the visitor to explore without being reminded of the proximity to the area just beyond.

PE5 A sense of enclosure

➤ A SENSE OF ENCLOSURE CAN HELP MAKE A PLACE COMFORTING
AND DISTINCT.

Some small spaces succeed by providing a sense of enclosure. The enclosure is a protective layer; it offers visual separation, which, in turn, affords privacy and distinctness. Effective enclosures enable one to track the area beyond while feeling safely tucked within.

Enclosures come in many forms. Some require minimal effort, such as the space created by low-branching trees or a narrow shrub planting. Some enclosures are more elaborate, such as the tradition of a sitting room within the garden (*berså*) found in Scandinavian countries. Many courtyards serve as enclosures, providing clear separation and a distinct place that is interesting to explore.

The Scandinavian garden room or berså.

A partial enclosure, such as a buffer that establishes protection from neighboring land uses, can also play a powerful role. For example, a tree buffer at the edge of a park or between a highway and a residential area can help clarify what lies within and what is beyond. Such buffers do not need to be large to fulfill their purposes as distinct, as partitions, and as comforting.

The feeling of an enclosure can be achieved in a courtyard by high hedges along a path, and even by a few trees in a larger area.

Part IV

With People in Mind

Design and management of natural settings are human activities that lead to changes to the environment. Those changes, in turn, impact people in numerous and pervasive ways. People's lives are affected by modification of ecosystems, conversion of forestland, alteration of transportation routes, creation of nature trails, and many other changes to the environment. The impacts can be deeply felt even when the change is relatively small; the removal of a single tree, for example, may cause considerable grief, while the addition of a tree may cause great joy.

The focus of the previous chapters was on changes to natural settings that consider human dimensions while also being environmentally sound. This last part of the book shifts attention from changes made to settings to the process of making decisions. The way design and management decisions are reached has a great deal to do with people's response to the changes.

Planners, designers, and managers all have their tales of woe concerning individuals or groups who have unleashed their objections to some well-intended proposal or decision. Citizens have their own tales to tell about unresponsive officials. These stories are rarely bland, and they do not typically focus on the best in any of the parties. Characteristically, criticism is expressed in terms of the presumed lack of intellectual capacity of the other side. After all, if "they" had the knowledge and insight that "we" possess, they would reach the same conclusion.

Generally, design and management decisions related to the nearby natural environment call upon a variety of experts and expertise. Knowledge pertinent to such decisions is not the exclusive domain of the experts, however. Bits and pieces of relevant information are lodged in the minds of many. Reaching a solution that is acceptable, and even satisfying, is more likely if it draws on the collected wisdom of all concerned parties. Chapter 10, "Engaging People," explores some ways to obtain the diverse kinds of information that are required to reach a reasonable solution.

As is true of other parts of the book, "Engaging People" does not offer an exhaustive discussion of the subject. Its purpose is to highlight the importance of obtaining and incorporating input. The patterns offered are intended to show some ways that design and management decisions can draw on people's knowledge and help people understand the constraints of a situation.

In chapter 11, "Putting It Together," the focus is on how each of the patterns in the book speaks to the themes that were presented in previous chapters. The forty-five patterns are intended to be widely applicable to the many nearby natural settings that are part of people's daily lives. They provide a diverse collection of ways that some of the more desirable qualities of human beings can be called upon, fostered, and rewarded.

Chapter 10

Engaging People

"One size fits all" rarely provides a very good fit. A better fit requires accommodating to the many ways in which people differ. Some differences are due to the characteristics of a culture and even to the local history of a place. Others may have to do with the particular needs and inclinations of the people in an area. Without an exploration of local variations, the best laid plans and most creative solutions are vulnerable. This section looks at some ways to benefit from differences.

In chapter 2 we talked about differences in the ways experts and local citizens might see the same situation. Certainly, the nearby natural world is a case in point. It is too frequently the case that the public's concerns about the design and management of a natural setting are aired only when public participation is mandated, or when a situation has reached a point of divisiveness. Ideally, opportunities for engaging the local community would occur more routinely and readily. The intended users often have a great deal to contribute to the planning, design, and management of their environment.

The patterns in this chapter address the following issues:

- Participation can lead to unique solutions that speak to local needs and fit the local context.

- Genuine impact can lead to greater sense of ownership, stewardship, and community.

- People are sensitive to signs of making a difference.

- Information that is not understandable is unlikely to be a contribution.

When local needs and understanding are routinely incorporated in design and management the resulting solutions can be, and have been, far more satisfying for all concerned. For example, community partici-

pation in tree-planting programs has been found to enhance social identity, self-esteem, and territoriality. Furthermore, the impact of participation has been shown to extend even to those who were not directly involved but were aware that participation had been included in the decision-making process.

Grassroots efforts have often served to coalesce community resources and to challenge bureaucratic assumptions. While such efforts have at times had negative consequences—such as protecting self-interests at the expense of others—it would be unfortunate to dismiss this potentially useful human resource. The wisdom and concern that energize such efforts can be enormous assets. It is important to acknowledge the insights and perspectives of local groups and invite their participation in design and management.

To be effective, however, the participation needs to be designed in a way that recognizes the distinct perspectives of the public and the experts. There is a considerable literature that documents differences between decision makers and users, between those with design training and others, between managers and citizens. The information held by locals is no less pertinent than the information held by those who wield power, money, and scientific "truths." The discrepancies between what experts know and take for granted and what the public knows and holds dear must be examined. Incorporating participation is an effective way to recognize that experts and affected groups have different knowledge, perceptions, and needs. (See chapter 2, "Sharing Information.")

Many cases of public participation have left both citizens and professionals feeling frustrated and angered. Effective participation requires more than good intentions. All too often the public finds the information that is presented to be incomprehensible and overwhelming. To further complicate the situation, the forum for encouraging the exchange of information is often intimidating and baffling to the public. Formal public hearings may be particularly difficult devices for comfortable communication in either direction. Fortunately, there are many other options available; alternatives can also provide ways to gain much wider participation than is often the case.

Incorporating public input and citizen concerns would be a far simpler task if the public represented a single point of view. That is rarely the case. The "public" is many publics. Their perspectives are necessarily incomplete since they are based on different experiences and knowledge. Their perspectives are likely to clash since they are based on different needs and desires. Which is the "right" public to be heeded? Are there ways to learn about perspectives before there is a crisis, from the publics that are less likely to speak their minds? To explore these and related questions fully would require far more than a single chapter. On the other hand, some useful tools and techniques can be described briefly. It is our hope that even a very incomplete treatment of this important topic can serve as a starting point toward making public input a positive rather than a threatening experience.

This would be an important and hopeful step, since the process of trial and error is frequently an essential step in finding a good solution. Small experiments can be particularly useful in trying things out before introducing a massive change; they can be sensitive to local input and feedback. Many characteristics of small experiments, such as greater public involvement, attention to what works, and willingness to make changes, are important aspects of effective participation.

This chapter is divided into two parts, roughly related to *design* and *management*. Design requires anticipating what a place will be like in the future. Too often there are unwelcome surprises: "We had no idea it would be like that!" Amidst the hope and expectation that changes will bring improvements, there is often less attention to the things one takes for granted. People sometimes do not realize how important aspects of their existing setting are to them until they no longer have them. The patterns related to management address ways to encourage and sustain stewardship, permitting local individuals and groups an ongoing part in sustaining their own setting.

The patterns:

Design

EP:D1 *Start early, include many*
EP:D2 *Understandable information*
EP:D3 *Providing alternatives*
EP:D4 *The art of inviting feedback*

Management

EP:M1 *Opportunities for participation*
EP:M2 *Why should I read this?*
EP:M3 *Small experiments*

EP:D1 Start early, include many

➤ GENUINE PARTICIPATION NEEDS TO START EARLY AND REACH THE DIVERSE SEGMENTS OF THE POPULATION.

When should public input be sought? There are several factors that favor waiting until relatively late in the planning and design process before inviting participation. One of these is fear that the affected groups will be displeased about the changes that might take place. Another is that the planners or designers are not yet ready to let the public know what the changes will encompass. While those may be appropriate reasons for delays from an agency's perspective, such delays readily lead to community divisiveness and hostility.

For those who are likely to be affected by impending changes, there is a desire to be included early in the planning process. People want to know about decisions that may affect them, and—more than that—they are likely to want to take a part in finding solutions that speak to their setting and their concerns.

There are many ways to involve citizens in the planning of public parks and other civic improvements.

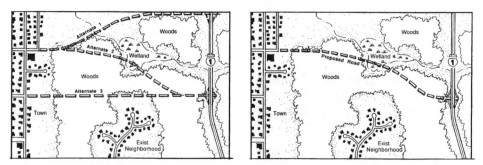

The proposed road project (left) is probably early enough in the planning stages to involve the public. By contrast, the project shown on the right is probably too far along to allow for meaningful public participation.

Involving people sooner necessarily means that many aspects of a solution will not yet have been worked out. Thus, by initiating participation at a relatively early stage, there is a greater chance that public input can have a genuine impact on the outcome. People welcome the opportunity to have their views heard; they have also been soured by being asked and then ignored.

Participation of citizens in the planning process does not guarantee public cooperation or approval, but not including the public can have dire consequences for public officials.

While there are important reasons for getting public input early in the process, there are also reasons to involve the public at many other times during planning and design. The next few patterns address a variety of formats that can be useful at different stages in the process.

It is unrealistic to think that participation will involve everyone who might be impacted by a change. Is it realistic, however, to think that the opinions of a few influential people in the community are appropriate and sufficient? Depending on the nature of a project, it is useful to think of ways to involve a wide spectrum of the public—or at least to provide the opportunity for their input. Once a situation is permitted to become divisive and friction in the community is hard to ignore, the various stakeholders are likely to take part in efforts to negotiate a solution. It would be better to consider those potentially affected groups without the pressure and polarization induced by conflict.

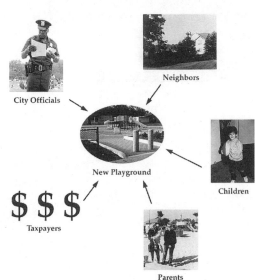

A wide variety of stakeholders should be involved in the planning of public spaces such as new playgrounds.

EP:D2 Understandable information

➤ MEANINGFUL PARTICIPATION REQUIRES INFORMATION THAT IS
READILY UNDERSTOOD.

Providing useful information to the public is much more difficult than
generally recognized. The cost of providing information that is not
understood can be substantial. These costs readily express themselves
in the form of frustration, distress, distrust, hostility, and a sense of
futility.

When those guiding the participation process are fearful of the public's reaction, they may be tempted to provide information that is overwhelming and too technical for the public to understand. While some
citizens may be daunted by material that is too difficult, others may
express their anger with little reservation. There is much more to be
gained by considering what information the public might perceive as
useful and helpful and by finding ways to communicate it so that a
meaningful exchange can take place.

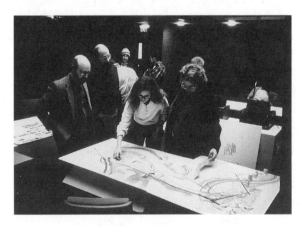

*Physical models can help
people imagine the setting.*

*Squiggles and pat-
terns can mean little
to non-designers. Site
plans can be difficult
to visualize in three
dimensions.*

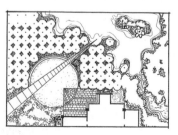

There is no guaranteed path to understandable information, but some approaches have a higher likelihood of success than others. Pictures can work wonders. Providing visual images of some possibilities can be very effective. But the key word is "can." Just because the information is visual does not mean it is understandable. Photographs of existing places are often helpful; artistic sketches might be less so, especially if they rely on a professional shorthand that is too abstract for people who are not trained in design. Similarly, even though site plans are visual, few people can imagine them as three-dimensional.

Since it is difficult for people to imagine settings that are not yet in existence, physical models can be helpful. They can be photographed or used interactively. People find such models useful and understandable even if they lack detail. For example, layers of foamboard glued together to approximate structures can be easily interpreted. Computer simulation methods can also be effective for presenting a future environment in three dimensions.

Simple models convey the appropriate level of information for many public participation efforts (top row). Detailed models, on the other hand, require a larger investment of time and money without a corresponding increase in public understanding of the project (bottom row).

This series of computer-enhanced images shows the impact of different types of development on a stretch of rural highway.

A lack of detail can be helpful. When a great deal of detail is present-ed, the public might suspect that critical decisions have already been made and that, the desire to obtain local input is not genuine. Detail can also focus the discussion at an inappropriate level of analysis. For exam-ple, architectural detail of a new building or decisions about particular plantings may be appropriate later in the decision process but would be distracting when decisions about siting have not yet been made.

People are often reassured if they can place themselves in the context of the planned change. This might involve finding one's neighborhood or an orienting landmark on a map of the proposed project. Rather than considering citizens' efforts to find such information as parochial, it is appropriate to encourage them to take the time to feel comfortable with the material.

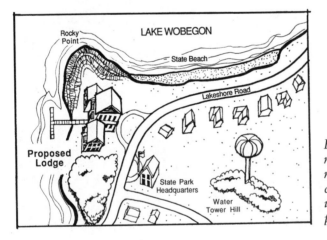

By highlighting familiar neighborhoods and land-marks, development plans can help local residents understand the context of proposed changes.

There are also times when direct exposure, rather than simulation, is an effective way to achieve understanding about an impending project. A field trip can have many benefits. It can provide the opportunity to walk through an area, explore the results of previous efforts, and discuss implications of alternative solutions.

Field trips can help focus discussion on the place rather than on ideological differences between stakeholder groups.

EP:D3 Providing alternatives

➤ PEOPLE RESPOND MORE USEFULLY IF PROVIDED REASONABLE CHOICES.

The purpose of providing alternatives is not to force a choice or pick a "winner." Rather, alternatives should provide some notions of what is feasible; they can help to communicate the range of issues that need to be considered. The final solution is likely to incorporate pieces of several alternatives. As such, the solution cannot be anticipated—it is emergent, permitting both local input and the designer's creative reactions to help give it shape.

Alternative plaza designs with and without a proposed sculpture.

Presenting several alternatives to the public in their full complexity may be overwhelming. Furthermore, if each alternative is difficult to understand, such a format could defeat the intention of permitting the public to consider a range of solutions. Instead, it often is effective to present the alternatives in terms of separable, distinct chunks that could be combined in different ways.

For example, rather than presenting three big solutions for a park design (emphasizing sports facilities, natural areas, or an interface with commercial facilities), it is useful to provide images of the pieces or ele-

Having people respond to a variety of elements rather than to a final site plan allows the designer to weave those elements into a workable solution.

ments that could be combined in a variety of ways in a final outcome. These might include bleachers, baseball diamond, tennis courts, concession stands, parkside boutiques, a grove of shade trees, trails and seating areas, and picnic shelters. By providing choices, one permits the participants to see a range of what could be done.

If citizens are asked to respond to choices, it is crucial that their feedback be a reasonable indicator of their sentiments. That means that there need to be a few examples of a proposed alternative rather than the dependence on a single instance. Providing a single version can easily lead to misleading or confusing results. For example, if a single image of a grove of shade trees is presented, in a rectilinear pattern, surrounded by pavement, it may be difficult to know whether the public's response is to the trees, their arrangement, or the setting. Having a second example that also includes shade trees, but in a distinctly different arrangement, would permit comparison of the responses.

Often it is necessary to include several instances of the same type of scene in order to determine the attributes to which people are responding.

EP:D4 The art of inviting feedback

➤ The format for getting feedback has to be friendly and appropriate.

Many well-intended efforts to involve the public yield little useful information and leave many bad feelings. While some citizens are articulate, fearless public speakers, and quite clear on what options are available, they are a rarity. That does not mean that the majority of the public is incompetent or ignorant or useless. Rather, one must find ways to obtain public input that are compatible with the public's strengths and concerns.

Going to where the people are is one way to elicit feedback. In this instance, residents attending a community festival are being asked to choose park elements from examples shown on photo boards.

The emphasis here is on obtaining responses from diverse segments of the public in ways that do not result in extensive efforts on the part of a few citizens. People want to be asked about the information they have and about their concerns and preferences, but they can be easily put off by how they are asked. Satisfying approaches to public participation in planning and design provide information about constraints but also assure that the public's viewpoints and wisdom are incorporated in the process.

"What do you want" is often a doomed question. Many people have no notion how to answer such a question. Others may tell you what they want, but it is likely to be unrealistic. By asking the question, then, one easily intimidates those who lack a ready answer and falsely raises the hopes of those whose requests cannot be met.

By contrast, using photographs to present solutions and asking people to indicate their preferences works very well. That is a task that is not only manageable but even enjoyable. Models also provide a way to show alternatives and to elicit a quick indication of preference. Through the process of seeing alternatives, citizens can learn about the range of possibilities and can contribute their concerns (see "Readings").

The first five pages of the booklet consist of photographs. The pictures were taken in many places and are intended as suggestions of how this area could look in the future. Please think of these scenes in terms of places that you might see in the North Main/Huron River Study Area.

For EACH photograph, please indicate how much you would like the kind of setting it represents *if it were in this area*. The more you like the scene for this area, the higher the number you would circle on the scale beneath the photograph, so that:

Preference:
1 = not at all
2 = a little
3 = somewhat
4 = quite a bit
5 = very much

A photo questionnaire is a readily understandable method for discovering people's preference for particular environmental elements.

Many other formats can be used to obtain public response, and often a mixture of approaches is needed (see "Readings"). Instead of a formal public hearing, for example, citizens can be divided into small working groups to discuss alternatives. Feedback from each group can be obtained by having a group member report to the larger group, by asking the group as a whole or its members to complete a short survey, or by having a designated person record the group's discussion.

Models, especially those with movable parts, are useful for obtaining feedback from people of all ages.

EP:M1 Opportunities for participation

➤ PERMITTING LOCAL INVOLVEMENT NEEDS TO BE AN ONGOING PART
OF MANAGEMENT.

Here are some statistics from one organization (The Nature Conservancy), in one state (Illinois), for one year (1996):

   Number of volunteers who worked in 1996 — 5,602
   Number of hours spent doing ecological management work — 56,986
   Number of hours spent doing administrative work — 3,696
   Number of special events held — 101
   Number of people who attended these events — 2,248
   Number of acres under management — 67,302

Clearly, the environment benefits from this outpouring of effort. Less tangible are the benefits to the participants, but the personal gains are many and far-reaching. One would hardly expect ventures such as the Volunteer Stewardship Network to persist and grow if the participants did not find satisfaction in those activities. In fact, local people participate in the well-being of their environments in thousands of settings. Programs vary along many dimensions, including the nature of the tasks involved, the organizational characteristics, and the numbers of volunteers and their experience.

Volunteers can make important contributions to park maintenance.

Newspapers, newsletters, and magazines are rich in anecdotal evidence of the significance to the participants and the community of programs that draw on local human resources. Research results also point to participants' sense of accomplishment, joy in learning new things, pride in contributing to the appearance of their neighborhood, and feeling that the enormity of environmental degradation need not be so hopeless.

Wonderful as they can be, it is important to acknowledge that volunteer programs present a number of challenges. Sufficient organization and leadership are needed to sustain well-intended programs. Unfortunately, agencies often lack the resources required for organizing and supervising such activities. They also may not have the time it takes to build a relationship and understand what skills volunteers bring to the situation. Without the necessary guidance, volunteers can become discouraged when they do not know what to do next or inadvertently cause damage by actions that are contrary to the organization's plan.

Such challenges are surmountable however, and the consequences of permitting local involvement can provide benefits to the land, the agency, and the participants. Opportunities for local participation are numerous. Residents in apartment complexes can participate in the greening of their neighborhood by being allowed to grow plants outside

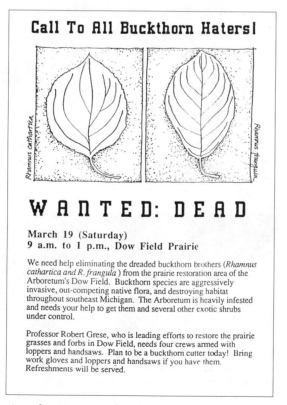

An advertisement that suggests that local involvement can be fun.

Grassroots efforts are often the catalyst for increased community participation in management of local parks.

their own dwelling. Residents can be invited to participate in maintaining parks or trails in neighborhood parks. Local talent can be tapped for helping with youth outdoor programs. Although it requires flexibility and ingenuity, utilizing such resources can create a situation where everyone wins.

Here are some examples of involving volunteers, in some instances jointly with staff, in local activities. Top: A tree planting project (left) and botanical garden maintenance (right). Bottom: Helping with a prairie burn (left) and park maintenance (right). The children in the last example learn about historic farming practices while helping to maintain a demonstration garden.

EP:M2 Why should I read this?

➤ BROCHURES AND PAMPHLETS ARE MORE LIKELY TO BE READ IF THEY ARE
USER FRIENDLY.

Even when people have been provided with all the information they
could possibly need, they often don't follow the instructions. The fact
that needed information is right in front of them does not necessarily
make it readily available. There are many reasons *not* to read or heed
material and not to follow instructions. Rather than accusing people of
incompetence, it may be more appropriate to examine ways to make
information relevant and useful.

The pattern on understandable information (EP:D2) addresses the
idea of providing images of places that are not yet existent. The emphasis in this pattern is on the many occasions when brochures or pamphlets
are used for informing the public (for example, about curbside recycling,
a particular nature area, or ways to manage gypsy moth infestations).
Such materials frequently fail to achieve their intent.

*Even government officials can
be skeptical about why they
should read something.*

A few simple ideas may be useful when preparing such material:

Holding back: The temptation to include too much information is
enormous. The difficulty is that the quantity does not seem excessive to
the person who is already informed. If anything, the information provider may feel frustrated by how little of the important information is
being conveyed. To the novice recipient, by contrast, the material may be
overwhelming and the temptation not to look at it at all substantial.

The left bulletin strikes an appropriate balance between text and graphics. The right one, on the other hand, may provide more technical information than many readers would find manageable.

The "where-they're-at" principle. If a quick glance suggests to the reader that the information is "the same old stuff," the likelihood of a second glance is small. If it seems technical and difficult, that, too, will end the process. The material has a greater chance of being read if the reader's existing knowledge and concerns are recognized and incorporated. Since users of the material will have differing prior knowledge, written materials cannot be specifically geared to each person's experience. Nonetheless, one can ask readers to consider their own perceptions of a situation or draw on likely common experiences that pertain to the situation. Rather than assuming that readers are hungry for the information that is provided, attention to their knowledge, worries, and circumstances can lead to more effective information exchange.

Telling a story. Material intended for younger audiences often is engaging and easy to grasp, but, for some reason, adults are treated differently. Chances are that attractive pages, appropriate graphics, understandable prose, and intriguing content will more effectively communicate material even to adult audiences. The notions of understanding and exploration are neither specific to younger people nor pertinent exclusively to environments. A story has two crucial aspects in terms of attracting and holding people's interest. First, it provides concrete imagery. Second, it creates both uncertainty and the promise of resolving it. Material structured in this way is engaging and encourages exploration.

Environmental information should incorporate the audience's existing experience.

Sometimes adults are afraid to ask questions. This brochure addresses that issue in a humorous, nonthreatening manner.

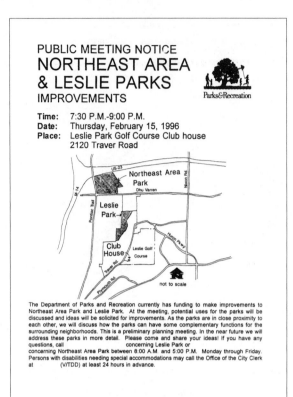

PUBLIC MEETING NOTICE
NORTHEAST AREA & LESLIE PARKS
IMPROVEMENTS

Parks&Recreation

Time: 7:30 P.M.-9:00 P.M.
Date: Thursday, February 15, 1996
Place: Leslie Park Golf Course Club house
2120 Traver Road

not to scale

The Department of Parks and Recreation currently has funding to make improvements to Northeast Area Park and Leslie Park. At the meeting, potential uses for the parks will be discussed and ideas will be solicited for improvements. As the parks are in close proximity to each other, we will discuss how the parks can have some complementary functions for the surrounding neighborhoods. This is a preliminary planning meeting. In the near future we will address these parks in more detail. Please come and share your ideas! If you have any questions, call   concerning Leslie Park or
concerning Northeast Area Park between 8:00 A.M. and 5:00 P.M. Monday through Friday. Persons with disabilities needing special accommodations may call the Office of the City Clerk at   (V/TDD) at least 24 hours in advance.

Many citizens would find this announcement less than inviting.

EP:M3 Small experiments

➤ TRYING THINGS OUT IN A QUICK, SAFE, AND SIMPLE WAY CAN FACILITATE
GOOD DECISIONS.

Small ideas...

*...can lead to
big adventures.*

*Planting a
seedling...*

*...can create a
forest.*

Often when one is not quite sure what to do, trying something out and seeing what happens can be a big help. Such small experiments are so common that they seem unremarkable. Yet they are a powerful means for sharpening our intuitions, overcoming indecision, and testing ideas without undue baggage. These tentative efforts are not intended for yielding definitive answers. Yet the accumulation of partial and imperfect answers can contribute to greater understanding as well as to new explorations.

Small experiments can also be a powerful tool in less personal contexts. They can provide a way for citizens and experts to work together, for local talent to help develop solutions that maintain local identity, for innovations that are appropriate to the context. The key ideas in small experiments derive from those two words: *small* and *experiment*. The intention is to keep the efforts at a modest scale: small enough to be relatively manageable; small enough that mistakes are not overwhelming; small enough that, in due time, one will have the energy to tackle yet another small experiment. The notion of experiment suggests a quest, a search for an answer.

A small experiment stands in marked contrast to large-scale research. Research is often intimidating and costly, with outcomes that may be difficult to comprehend. The results may fail to speak to the intended purposes despite a major commitment of time and resources. To the traditional researcher the lack of ideal conditions precludes definitive answers. Small experiments, by contrast, provide a way to address some of the intended purposes within the constraints of the existing context. There is no assumption of perfection, but rather a sense of getting closer to a useful understanding.

Smallness can express itself in terms of a variety of dimensions. The physical area can be kept small—for example, by converting turf grass to a wildflower meadow in only one section of a park. An experiment

Before   *After*

can be tried on a limited basis—for example, introducing an effort to have the public maintain flower beds in only one or two parks rather than throughout the system. The number of people involved in the experiment can also be kept small—for example, testing new orienting material with a small group of visitors.

While small experiments are necessarily modest, incomplete, and imperfect, they can nonetheless be extraordinarily useful. Furthermore, one can gain information without costly commitments that may need to be undone. That is not to say, however, that anything goes. The following are topics that should be considered in planning an effective experiment:

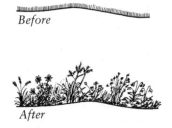

Before

After

Goal or purpose. The small experiment needs to be about something—not everything. It should have a focus. A clear question provides motivation; it also helps in formulating a study that is likely to yield useful results. For example, the goals in converting a small area from turf grass to a wildflower meadow might be to increase environmental diversity and to educate passersby. Or the goal may be to have the management staff find out if they can use volunteers effectively. The single most damaging problem in attempts to do small experiments stems from devoting too little effort to thinking through what one hopes to learn.

Tracking. Small experiments require one to be mindful of what is going on. They depend on efforts to be somewhat observant and systematic, to keep track of key aspects of the situation. The information gathering needs to be manageable. Too much information can be overwhelming; too little information can also be problematic. The amount and form of information to be gathered is thus important to weigh before launching the study. For example, a project that explores having community participation in the maintenance of flower beds could involve weekly monitoring of how well the beds are maintained using a quick checklist to record the presence of wilted flowers, damaged plants, etc. It is also useful to consider whether some information may be available that would not require additional cost or effort. For example, information about the numbers of people enrolling in a program, requesting material, or attending an event is often easily obtained.

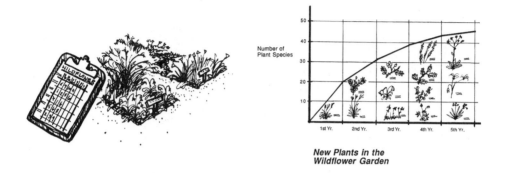

New Plants in the Wildflower Garden

Dissemination. To be useful, the results of the small experiment need to be shared. Depending on the context, shared information can let participants know that their input made a difference; it provides an opportunity to let a wider audience know what was learned and what next steps might be taken as a result. Effective ways to communicate the outcomes will also vary with the circumstances. Sometimes inclusion in a newsletter provides a useful way to reach the intended audience. A mailing to people who are involved with the project may also be appropriate.

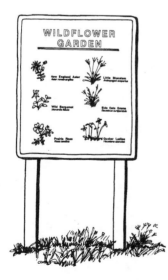

In the wildflower meadow example, the shared information could include signs that indicate the increased species diversity. In other instances, guided walks through an area can serve to inform visitors of the results. Sharing seeds and plants can also be an appreciated way to share the results of a small experiment. Whatever the approach, it is important that the results are shared and that the form of communication is likely to be user friendly. Once again, as with other patterns concerning the sharing of information, it is important to consider how the message is conveyed.

Chapter 11

Putting It Together

As we said at the start: This book is about nature, but it is also about people. It is about the way the natural environment can foster well-being and can enhance people's ability to function effectively. The underlying purpose of the book is to explore the design and management of nearby natural areas in ways that are beneficial for people and are likely to win their support, appreciation, and enthusiasm.

Our emphasis throughout the book has been on the interplay between the setting and people. Our position has been that maintaining a concern for people need not replace a concern for the environment; at the same time, ignoring the needs and inclinations of people can do great harm to humans and, ultimately, to the environment as well. The purpose of this last chapter is to revisit the themes of the book in a way that cuts across the previous chapters and sections. We take this second look from the perspective of people's inclinations, reiterating the concerns for design and management with people in mind.

Where Is "Nearby Nature"?

This book has focused on everyday natural settings, on natural places that are nearby. Such places might be quite small, but they can also have considerable extent, as is the case with regional or "metro" parks. Nearby nature can be in an urban setting, but it is not limited to cities. It can be near one's home or workplace, near hospitals, schools, or other institutions. Nearby nature is where one might want to take a walk or hike, or it may provide an opportunity to sit and observe or perhaps even consider weighty matters on one's mind.

The many patterns discussed in the previous chapters are intended to be applicable to a wide range of settings and situations. In part II, "Meeting the Challenges," we looked at issues related to fears and preferences, way-finding, and restorative environments, all topics that are pertinent to many kinds of nearby natural settings. For example, simplifying way-finding is equally important in a park or on a corporate campus. Similarly, people's fears can get in the way of the use of places small or large. In part III, "Design and Management Opportunities," we talked about the importance of having a sense of enclosure, about views, and points of interest. Such patterns are equally pertinent to consider in the context of industrial landscaping or a neighborhood park. There is indeed a huge range of opportunities for providing and improving nearby nature settings. The longings for such settings, unfortunately, often go unfulfilled.

For Whom?

Implicit in our discussion of nearby nature is that there are people in the equation. These are people who find themselves in nearby natural settings for many reasons and to pursue a host of activities; children, teens, and adults of all ages; the ailing and the recovering, as well as the healthy; neighbors, visitors, and even those whose work involves such settings. They are people who come on foot, by bike, in a car, or in a wheelchair. They are individuals with vast specialized knowledge about ecology, botany, planning, design, and many other areas that pertain to the natural settings. They are also people whose knowledge is based on no more than prior experience and those who have little of that.

Even though people come in all sizes, shapes, and varieties, there are similarities in their preferences and needs. How those are expressed, however, varies across cultures, people, and time. Given such diversity, it would hardly be appropriate to suggest universal solutions for all contexts and groups. Though the solutions cannot be applied universally, the problems they address are broadly relevant and vital to consider. The patterns presented in this book speak to those problems and circumstances.

Some Major Themes

Though people differ in many respects, there is an aspect of humans that is perhaps more universal than one might wish to acknowledge. People can be incredibly frustrating to deal with. Seemingly reasonable people can at times be exasperating. Sometimes people can be difficult, annoying, and uncooperative. Such qualities are neither rare nor restricted to any segment of the population. They can be found in experts in a field as well as ordinary citizens, in adults as well as children, in people of any ethnicity, with more or less education, with or without resources. One can hit upon those qualities in dealings with individuals or groups. This negative side of the species has many consequences: Great intentions go unappreciated, fond hopes get shattered, and beautiful places are vandalized.

There are numerous reasons for such behavior. Some of them are directly related to what this book is about. We have listed only four potential factors here. Those four, however, provide a framework for looking at the forty-five patterns introduced in earlier pages. Briefly stated, people are often more difficult and problematic when:

- The environment hinders or blocks their **understanding**.

- The environment lacks opportunities for **exploration**.

- The environment fails to foster experiences that are **restful and enjoyable**.

- People feel their **participation** is not welcome.

These are not new themes. They have been with us throughout these pages (see chapter 2, "Some Human Characteristics"). While stated as separate themes, in many cases their ramifications are interrelated. As such, many of the patterns apply to more than one of these themes. We have, however, tried to place each pattern in a single category, although there are a few exceptions (and one pattern applies to all four of these categories). Let us look at each of these four themes and consider the patterns that are directly applicable.

Understanding

Being able to make sense of one's environment is critical to feeling competent, to feeling less fearful and overwhelmed. Many of the patterns speak to ways to help people comprehend a natural area. We have grouped them under three headings.

Creating Regions and Providing Distinctive Elements

Understanding is fostered by making the environment readily interpretable. Having a sense of the important pieces and how they relate to each other makes it easier to grasp the setting. Choice points and landmarks are important components of an understandable environment. Here are some of the patterns that address those issues:

COHERENT AREAS (P1)
➤ *A small number of coherent areas makes a setting easier to understand.*

REGIONS (WF:D1)
➤ *Coherent regions are helpful in way-finding.*

GATEWAYS NEED PARTITIONS (G1)
➤ *Partitions create opportunities for gateways.*

LANDMARKS (WF:D2)
➤ *Landmarks are most useful in way-finding when they are distinctive and not too many.*

THE TRAIL'S PATH (T4)
➤ *Helping people stay oriented is an important function of a trail.*

ORIENTATION FOR THE NEW VISITOR (WF:M1)
➤ *Key decision points need to be easily identified.*

Providing Supplementary Cues and Information

Understanding is enhanced through other forms of information than what the environment itself provides. Often such supplementary information is in the forms of signs, brochures, or maps. Several patterns are related to providing such information in a useful fashion.

UNDERSTANDABLE INFORMATION (EP:D2)
➤ *Meaningful participation requires information that is readily understood.*

WHY SHOULD I READ THIS? (EP:M2)
➤ *Brochures and pamphlets are more likely to be read if they are user friendly.*

LABELS AND SYMBOLS (WF:M3)
➤ *Maps are more helpful if the information is where one needs it.*

MAPPING FOR THE MIND'S EYE (WF:M2)
➤ *Avoiding the accuracy hang-up leads to a more easily remembered map.*

PATHS AND SIGNS (WF:D3)
➤ *Getting there and back can be aided by paths and signs.*

WHICH WAY IS NORTH? (WF:M4)
➤ *Align a posted map with the viewer's position.*

Compatibility with Human Biases

The patterns grouped under this heading have in common that they deal with the relation of some basic human characteristics to environmental contexts. Certain environmental qualities increase people's sense of comfort and trust, especially under circumstances when they might be fearful. (These patterns may be less applicable for people with a great deal of pertinent experience; comparably, the issue of understanding the environment would be less urgent when one already has a great deal of relevant knowledge.)

ENHANCING FAMILIARITY (F2)
➤ *Familiarity helps people feel more comfortable.*

HUMAN SIGN (F3)
➤ *Although indications of human presence can be a source of concern, human sign is often reassuring.*

WOOD, STONE, AND OLD (R4)
➤ *The choice of materials can enhance restoration.*

A SENSE OF ENCLOSURE (PE5)
➤ *A sense of enclosure can make a place comforting and distinct.*

OPENINGS (P5)
➤ *Openings in the woods are comforting both when one is in them and when one can look into them.*

THE TRAIL SURFACE (T3)
➤ *Trail surfaces are important, both visually and functionally.*

SMOOTH GROUND (P2)
➤ *Ground texture impacts preference.*

Exploration

Humans are seekers. Settings that provide opportunities for people to venture out and explore are likely to be cherished. Exploration is enhanced by hints in the environment that offer possibilities for discovery and adventure. But exploration is by no means limited to the physical aspects of finding new places. A great deal of people's exploration comes from considering options, wondering, and imagining. The exploration patterns are grouped in three categories:

A Chance to See What's There

Several of the patterns concern ways to provide information about what lies ahead. Points of access enhance understanding as well as facilitating exploration. Here are some examples:

ORIENTATION FOR THE NEW VISITOR (WF:M1)
➤ *Key decision points need to be easily identified.*

VISUAL ACCESS (F1)
➤ *Visual access increases confidence.*

GATEWAYS AND ORIENTATION (G2)
➤ *A gateway provides information about what lies ahead.*

VIEWS, LARGE AND SMALL (T2)
➤ *What can be seen from the trail makes all the difference.*

GUIDING THE EYE (VV2)
➤ *A captivating view provides information about where to look.*

POINTS OF INTEREST (T5)
➤ *Stopping points along the way can provide opportunities for resting and observing.*

Around the Bend

Information that is just beyond, discernible but not quite present, is difficult to resist. It invites exploration.

THE VIEW THROUGH THE GATEWAY (G3)
➤ *A well-designed gateway can provide both information and mystery.*

MYSTERY (P3)
➤ *Mystery encourages exploration.*

TRAILS, NARROW AND CURVING (T1)
➤ *The promise of discovering what lies just beyond the bend in the road greatly increases preference.*

A SENSE OF DEPTH (P4)
➤ *Layers and landmarks enhance the sense of depth.*

The Mind's View

The conceptual view, the mind's exploration, is triggered by suggestions of what might be. Seeing only a small part of a larger piece or having some indication of places that are not immediately evident inspires the quest to discover. Several of the patterns discuss ways that the environment can foster such exploration.

MORE THAN MEETS THE EYE (VV3)
➤ *A vista engages the imagination.*

WANDERING IN SMALL SPACES (R2)
➤ *Even a small space, if it has extent, can constitute a whole different world.*

ENOUGH TO LOOK AT (VV1)
➤ *A vista is more engrossing if it has extent.*

THINK VIEW (VV4)
➤ *Consider opportunities for providing views.*

Restful and Enjoyable

Early in the book we discussed the concept of mental fatigue, a state of mind many people seem to experience all too frequently. Trying to pack too much into the day, even if the activities are in themselves enjoyable or interesting, can lead to a tired mind. "Time out" helps in regaining a sense of peacefulness. But some kinds of time out seem more likely to be restorative than others. Considerable research indicates that nature places and activities in natural settings are particularly effective. Several of the patterns listed in this chapter under "Compatibility with Human Biases" (the third set under "Understanding") suggest configurations that help with restoration. The patterns listed here all directly address those concerns as well:

QUIET FASCINATION (R1)
➤ *Natural settings can fill the mind and enhance restoration.*

WANDERING IN SMALL SPACES (R2)
➤ *Even a small space, if it has extent, can constitute a whole different world.*

SEPARATION FROM DISTRACTION (R3)
➤ *The sense of being in a different world is easily undermined by intrusions and distractions.*

THE VIEW FROM THE WINDOW (R5)
➤ *Even if one is not in a setting, it can have restorative benefits.*

TREES (PE1)
➤ *Trees help make special places.*

THE WATER'S EDGE (PE2)
➤ *The treatment of the water's edge impacts how the water is perceived.*

BIG SPACES (PE3)
➤ *Big areas become more interesting if divided.*

SMALL SPACES (PE4)
➤ *To be highly prized, places need not be large.*

Meaningful Participation

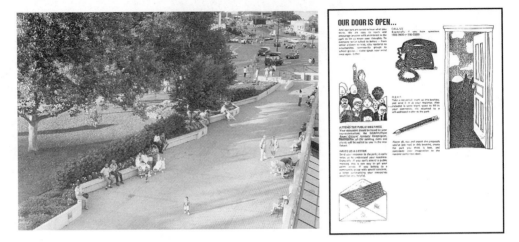

Often the reason people seem to be so disagreeable has to do with their own sense of frustration and annoyance with the circumstances around them. It seems to be a human quality that one prefers to be treated as if one is capable of understanding and can make a difference. People appreciate being asked about their views, having the sense that officials listen to them, that people in authority recognize that they may have something worthwhile to say. Those in authority are also human, of course. They too appreciate being listened to and being treated with respect. Such concerns run deep in humans; they are genuine, pervasive, and far-reaching—they are also frequently ignored. For many reasons, practical as well as moral and conceptual, it is appropriate to consider patterns that encourage including people in the design and management of their nearby natural world.

CHECK IT OUT (WF:M5)
➤ *Reactions from potential users can lead to surprising insights.*

OPPORTUNITIES FOR PARTICIPATION (EP:M1)
➤ *Permitting local involvement needs to be an ongoing part of management.*

START EARLY, INCLUDE MANY (EP:D1)
➤ *Genuine participation needs to start early and reach the diverse segments of the population.*

UNDERSTANDABLE INFORMATION (EP:D2)
➤ *Meaningful participation requires information that is readily understood.*

PROVIDING ALTERNATIVES (EP:D3)
➤ *People respond more usefully if provided reasonable choices.*

THE ART OF INVITING FEEDBACK (EP:D4)
➤ *The format for getting feedback has to be friendly and appropriate.*

The Final Pattern

There is one pattern we did not yet include, though it pertains to all four sections. It deserves a place of its own, rather than being repeated in each of the four. It is a pattern that is widely applicable. It has great potential for increasing understanding, for permitting exploration, for drawing on people's strengths, and for leading to solutions that are locally responsive.

SMALL EXPERIMENTS (EP:M3)
➤ *Trying things out in a quick, safe, and simple way can facilitate good decisions.*

Perhaps the following story (Skelton 1994) can put many of these thoughts together. It is a story about a park outside Gracie Mansion, the residence of the mayor of New York City. The Department of Parks and Recreation gardener assigned to the park, Bernadette Cozart, noticed a number of teens who preferred hanging out in the park to going to school. She became acquainted with them. She reports, "I started giving them shovels and rakes, and noticed they were really interested." Seeing their interest, she "struck a deal with them. They would return to classes, and in return, they could work with her after school each day to plant a garden. Cozart secured a grant to pay the teens small salaries, and gave each a patch of garden to tend. . . . They left the project with the respect of the people living nearby—as well as paid work experience and a skill" (p. 16).

As with many small experiments, the original intent of this project was to deal with a problem rather than to learn something that could have broader applications. It was also implemented on a sufficiently small scale that systematic record keeping was not essential. Nonetheless, the project produced results that are shareable and pertinent to other settings. They are also inspiring.

Was that a unique event? Fortunately, such stories can be told about many places, big and small. They involve environmental design and management. They include ecological restoration, tree maintenance, and a great variety of other activities. The striking part of each story is that the benefits extend far beyond the activity itself. While the setting benefits, so do people. The people who benefit are not only those who participate but also many others whose environment is changed by the activities. This book was written in the belief that the sum of many such small experiments, sensitive to the needs of both people and the environment, can change the world.

Appendix: Matrix of Patterns and Themes

The patterns are listed here chapter by chapter. In addition, the overarching themes introduced in the last chapter are indicated for each pattern.

The themes:

1: The importance of **understanding**
2: The need for **exploration**
3: Having a **restful and enjoyable** environment
4: Opportunities for **meaningful participation**

Part II Meeting the Challenges

Chapter 3 Fears and Preferences

Pattern	Description	1. Understanding	2. Exploration	3. Restful	4. Participation
F1 Visual access	➤ *Visual access increases confidence.*	X			
F2 Enhancing familiarity	➤ *Familiarity helps people feel more comfortable.*	X			
F3 Human sign	➤ *Although indications of human presence can be a source of concern, human sign is often reassuring.*	X			
P1 Coherent areas	➤ *A small number of coherent areas makes a setting easier to understand.*	X			
P2 Smooth ground	➤ *Ground texture impacts preference.*	X			
P3 Mystery	➤ *Mystery encourages exploration.*		X		
P4 A sense of depth	➤ *Layers and landmarks enhance the sense of depth.*		X		
P5 Openings	➤ *Openings in the woods are comforting both when one is in them and when one can look into them.*	X			

Chapter 4 Way-finding

WF Design:

Pattern	Description	1. Understanding	2. Exploration	3. Restful	4. Participation
WF:D1 Regions	➤ *Coherent regions are helpful in way-finding.*	X			
WF:D2 Landmarks	➤ *Landmarks are most useful in way-finding when they are distinctive and not too many.*	X			
WF:D3 Paths and signs	➤ *Getting there and back can be aided by paths and signs.*	X			

		1. Understanding	2. Exploration	3. Restful	4. Participation
WF Maps:					
WF:M1 Orientation for the new visitor	➤ Key decision points need to be easily identified.	X	X		
WF:M2 Mapping for the mind's eye	➤ Avoiding the accuracy hang-up leads to a more easily remembered map.	X			
WF:M3 Labels and symbols	➤ Maps are more helpful if the information is where one needs it.	X			
WF:M4 Which way is north?	➤ Align a posted map with the viewer's position.	X			
WF:M5 Check it out	➤ Reactions from potential users can lead to surprising insights.				X

Chapter 5 Restorative Environments

		1. Understanding	2. Exploration	3. Restful	4. Participation
R1 Quiet fascination	➤ Natural settings can fill the mind and enhance restoration.			X	
R2 Wandering in small spaces	➤ Even a small space, if it has extent, can constitute a whole different world.		X	X	
R3 Separation from distraction	➤ The sense of being in a different world is easily undermined by intrusions and distractions.			X	
R4 Wood, stone, and old	➤ The choice of materials can enhance restoration.	X			
R5 The view from the window	➤ Even if one is not in a setting, it can have restorative benefits.			X	

Part III Design and Management Opportunities

Chapter 6 Gateways and Partitions

		1. Understanding	2. Exploration	3. Restful	4. Participation
G1 Gateways need partitions	➤ Partitions create opportunities for gateways.	X			
G2 Gateways and orientation	➤ A gateway provides information about what lies ahead.		X		
G3 The view through the gateway	➤ A well-designed gateway can provide both information and mystery.		X		

Chapter 7 Trails and Locomotion

		1. Understanding	2. Exploration	3. Restful	4. Participation
T1 Trails, narrow and curving	➤ The promise of discovering what lies just beyond the bend in the road greatly increases preference.		X		
T2 Views, large and small	➤ What can be seen from the trail makes all the difference.		X		
T3 The trail surface	➤ Trail surfaces are important, both visually and functionally.	X			
T4 The trail's path	➤ Helping people stay oriented is an important function of a trail.	X			
T5 Points of interest	➤ Stopping points along the way can provide opportunities for resting and observing.			X	

		1. Understanding	2. Exploration	3. Restful	4. Participation

Chapter 8 Views and Vistas

		1. Understanding	2. Exploration	3. Restful	4. Participation
VV1 Enough to look at	➤ *A vista is more engrossing if it has extent.*			X	
VV2 Guiding the eye	➤ *A captivating view provides information about where to look.*			X	
VV3 More than meets the eye	➤ *A vista engages the imagination.*			X	
VV4 Think view	➤ *Consider opportunities for providing views.*			X	

Chapter 9 Places and Their Elements

		1. Understanding	2. Exploration	3. Restful	4. Participation
PE1 Trees	➤ *Trees help make special places.*			X	
PE2 The water's edge	➤ *The treatment of the water's edge impacts how the water is perceived.*			X	
PE3 Big spaces	➤ *Big areas become more interesting if divided.*			X	
PE4 Small spaces	➤ *To be highly prized, places need not be large.*			X	
PE5 A sense of enclosure	➤ *A sense of enclosure can make a place comforting and distinct.*	X			

Part IV With People in Mind

Chapter 10 Engaging People

EP Design:

		1. Understanding	2. Exploration	3. Restful	4. Participation
EP:D1 Start early, include many	➤ *Genuine participation needs to start early and reach the diverse segments of the population.*				X
EP:D2 Understandable information	➤ *Meaningful participation requires information that is readily understood.*	X			X
EP:D3 Providing alternatives	➤ *People respond more usefully if provided reasonable choices.*				X
EP:D4 The art of inviting feedback	➤ *The format for getting feedback has to be friendly and appropriate.*				X

EP Management:

		1. Understanding	2. Exploration	3. Restful	4. Participation
EP:M1 Opportunities for participation	➤ *Permitting local involvement needs to be an ongoing part of management.*				X
EP:M2 Why should I read this?	➤ *Brochures and pamphlets are more likely to be read if they are user friendly.*	X			
EP:M3 Small experiments	➤ *Trying things out in a quick, safe, and simple way can facilitate good decisions.*	X	X	X	X

Readings: By Subject

General Texts

Alexander, C.; Ishikawa, S.; and Silverstein, M. (1977). *A pattern language.* New York: Oxford University Press.

Altman, I., and Zube, E. H. (1989). *Public places and spaces.* New York: Plenum Press.

Carr, S.; Francis, M.; Rivlin, L. G.; and Stone, A. M. (1992). *Public space.* Cambridge: Cambridge University Press.

Cooper-Marcus, C., and Sarkissian, W. (1986). *Housing as if people mattered: Site design guidelines for medium-density housing.* Berkeley: University of California Press.

Francis, M. (1987). "Urban open spaces." In E. H. Zube and G. T. Moore (eds.), *Advances in environment, behavior, and design,* vol. 1. New York: Plenum Press.

Hartig, T., and Evans, G. W. (1993). "Psychological foundations of nature experience." In T. Gärling and R. G. Golledge (eds.), *Behavior and environment: Psychological and geographical approaches.* Amsterdam: Elsevier Science Publishers.

Kaplan, R., and Kaplan, S. (1989). *The experience of nature: A psychological perspective.* New York: Cambridge Press. (Republished by Ulrich's, Ann Arbor, MI: 1996.)

McAndrew, F. T. (1993). *Environmental psychology.* Pacific Grove, CA: Brooks/Cole Publishing.

Neely, D., ed. (1994). *Social aspects of urban forestry.* (Journal of Arboriculture: A compendium, vol. 6). Savoy, IL: International Society of Arboriculture.

Pigram, J. J. (1993). "Human-nature relationships: leisure environments and natural settings." In T. Gärling and R. G. Golledge (eds.), *Behavior and environment: Psychological and geographical approaches.* Amsterdam: Elsevier Science Publishers.

Schroeder, H. W. (1989). Environment, behavior, and design research on urban forests. In E. H. Zube and G. T. Moore (eds.), *Advances in environment, behavior, and design,* vol. 2. New York: Plenum Press.

Part I: By Way of Explanation: People and Nature

Importance of Nature: Nature vs. Urban
(also see chapter 9, "Places and Their Elements")

Chenoweth, R. E., and Gobster, P. H. (1990). "The nature and ecology of aesthetic experiences in the landscape." *Landscape Journal* 9: 1–8.

Francis, M. (1987). "Meanings attached to a city park and a community garden in Sacramento." *Landscape Research* 12(1): 8–12.

Furbrey, R., and Goodchild, B. (1986). "Attitudes to environment." *Housing* 22(3): 20–21.

Herzog, T. R.; Kaplan, S.; and Kaplan, R. (1976). "The prediction of preference of familiar urban places." *Environment and Behavior* 8: 627–645.

Herzog, T. R.; Kaplan, S.; and Kaplan, R. (1982). "The prediction of preference for unfamiliar urban places." *Population and Environment* 5(1): 43–59.

Homel, R., and Burns, A. (1987). "Is this a good place to grow up in? Neighbourhood quality and children's evaluations." *Landscape and Urban Planning* 14: 101–116.

Kaplan, R. (1983). "The role of nature in the urban context." In I. Altman and J. F. Wohlwill (eds.), *Behavior and the natural environment*. New York: Plenum Press.

Kaplan, R. (1984). "Impact of urban nature: A theoretical analysis." *Urban Ecology* 8: 189–197.

Kaplan, S. (1987). "Mental fatigue and the designed environment." In J. Harvey and D. Henning (eds.), *Public environments*. Washington, DC: Environmental Design Research Association, pp. 55–60.

Kaplan, S.; Kaplan, R.; and Wendt, J. S. (1972). "Rated preference and complexity for natural and urban visual material." *Perception and Psychophysics* 12: 354–356.

Lewis, C. A. (1996). *Green nature/human nature: The meaning of plants in our lives*. Urbana: University of Illinois Press.

Nachmias, C., and Palen, J. (1986). "Neighborhood satisfaction, expectations, and urban revitalization." *Journal of Urban Affairs* 8(4): 51–62.

Platt, R. H.; Rowntree, R. A.; and Muick, P. C., eds. (1994). *The ecological city: Preserving and restoring urban diversity*. Amherst: University of Massachusetts Press.

Schroeder, H. W. (1989). "Environment, behavior, and design research on urban forests." In E. H. Zube and G. T. Moore (eds.), *Advances in environment, behavior, and design*, vol. 2. New York: Plenum Press, p. 90.

Schroeder, H. W. (1990). "Perceptions and preferences of urban forest users." *Journal of Arboriculture* 16(3): 58–61.

Ulrich, R. S. (1981). "Natural versus urban scenes: Some psychological effects." *Environment and Behavior* 13: 523–556.

Ulrich, R. S. (1986). "Human responses to vegetation and landscape." *Landscape and Urban Planning* 13: 29–44.

Ulrich, R. S., and Addoms, D. L. (1981). "Psychological and recreational benefits of a residential park." *Journal Leisure Research* 13: 43–65.

Wohlwill, J. F. (1983). "The concept of nature: A psychologist's view." In I. Altman and J. F. Wohlwill (eds.), *Behavior and the natural environment.* New York: Plenum Press, pp. 5–37.

Importance of Nearby Nature: Proximity

Brunson, L.; Kuo, F. E.; and Sullivan, W. C. (under review). "Sowing the seeds of community: Greening and gardening in inner-city neighborhoods." *American Journal of Community Psychology.*

Darragh, A. J.; Peterson, G. L.; and Dwyer, J. F. (1983). "Travel cost models at the urban scale." *Journal of Leisure Research* 15(2): 89–94.

Kaplan, R. (1985). "Nature at the doorstep: Residential satisfaction and the nearby environment." *Journal of Architectural and Planning Research* 2: 115–127.

Kaplan, R. (1992). "The psychological benefits of nearby nature." In D. Relf (ed.), *The role of horticulture in human well-being and social development.* Portland, OR: Timber Press.

Kaplan, R., and S. Kaplan. (1989). "Nearby nature." *The experience of nature.* New York: Cambridge Press, pp. 150–174. (Republished by Ulrich's, Ann Arbor, MI: 1996.)

Lieber, S. R., and Allton, D. J. (1983). "Modeling trail area evaluations in metropolitan Chicago." *Journal of Leisure Research* 15(3): 184–202.

Peterson, G. L.; Dwyer, J. F.; and Darragh, A. J. (1983). "A behavioral urban recreation site choice model." *Leisure Sciences* 6(1): 61–81.

Talbot, J. F., and Kaplan, R. (1991). "The benefits of nearby nature for elderly apartment residents." *International Journal of Aging and Human Development* 33: 119–130.

Young, R. A., and Flowers, M. L. (1982). *Users of an urban natural area: Their characteristics, use patterns, satisfactions, and recommendations.* Forestry research report 82–4. University of Illinois, Urbana-Champaign: Department of Forestry, Agricultural Experiment Station.

Importance of Nearby Nature: Benefits
(also see chapter 8, "Views and Vistas")

Adler, J. (1984). "Harvest comes to Brooklyn." *Newsweek,* October 15, p. 17.

Alexander, C.; Ishikawa S.; and Silverstein, M. (1977). "Pattern 60: Accessible green." *A pattern language.* New York: Oxford University Press, pp. 304–309.

Dwyer, J. F.; McPherson; E. G.; Schroeder, H. W.; and Rowntree, R. A. (1992). "Assessing the benefits and costs of the urban forest." *Journal of Arboriculture* 18(5): 227–234.

Dwyer, J. F., and Schroeder, H. W. (1994). "The human dimensions of urban forestry." *Journal of Forestry* 92(10): 12–15.

Dwyer, J. F.; Schroeder, H. W.; and Gobster, P. H. (1991). "The significance of urban trees and forests: Toward a deeper understanding of values." *Journal of Arboriculture* 17(10): 276–284.

Flagler, J., and Poincelot, R. P. (1994). *People-plant relationships: Setting research priorities.* New York: Food Products Press.

Kaplan, R. (1973). "Some psychological benefits of gardening." *Environment and Behavior* 5: 145–161.

Kaplan, R.; Bardwell, L. V.; Ford, H. A.; and Kaplan, S. (1996). "The corporate back-40: Employee benefits of wildlife enhancement efforts on corporate land." *Human Dimensions of Wildlife* 1(2): 1–13.

Kuo, F. E.; Sullivan, W. C.; Coley, R. L.; and Brunson, L. (under review). "Fertile ground for community: Inner-city neighborhood common spaces." *American Journal of Community Psychology.*

Malakoff, D. (1995). "What good is community greening?" *Community Greening Review* 5: 4–11.

Naimark, S. (1982). *A handbook of community gardening.* New York: Scribner.

National Gardening Association. (1985). *Special report on community gardening in the U.S.* Burlington, VT: National Gardening Association.

National Urban Forest Forum. (1988). *Shedding a few tears.* Washington, DC: American Forestry Association. January/February.

Talbot, J. F.; Bardwell, L. V.; and Kaplan, R. (1987). "The functions of urban nature: Uses and values of different types of urban nature settings." *Journal of Architecture and Planning Research* 4: 47–63.

Taylor, A. F.; Wiley, A.; Kuo, F. E.; and Sullivan, W. C. (1998). "Growing up in the inner city: Green spaces as places to grow." *Environment and Behavior* 30(1): 3–27.

Chapter 2: Some Human Characteristics

Information: Understanding and Exploration
(also see chapter 3, "Fears and Preferences")

Carr, S., and Lynch, K. (1981). "Open space: Freedom and control." In L. Taylor (ed.), *Urban open spaces.* New York: Rizzoli.

Kaplan, R., and Kaplan, S. (1989). *The experience of nature: A psychological perspective.* New York: Cambridge Press. (Republished by Ulrich's, Ann Arbor, MI: 1996.)

Kaplan, S. (1975). "An informal model for the prediction of preference." In E. H. Zube, R. O. Brush, and J. G. Fabos (eds.), *Landscape assessment: Values, perceptions and resources.* Stroudsburg, PA: Dowden, Hutchinson, and Ross, pp. 92–101.

Kaplan, S. (1985). "Cognition and affect in environmental learning." *Children's Environmental Quarterly* 2(3): 19–21.

Kaplan, S. (1988). "Perception and landscape: Conceptions and misconceptions." In J. L. Nasar (ed.), *Environmental aesthetics: Theory, research, and application*. New York: Cambridge University Press, pp. 45–55.

Kaplan, S., and Kaplan, R., eds. (1978). *Humanscape: Environments for people*. Belmont, CA: Duxbury. (Republished by Ulrich's, Ann Arbor, MI: 1982.)

The Psychological Costs of Managing Information
(also see chapter 5, "Restorative Environments")

Cohen, S. (1978). "Environmental load and the allocation of attention." In A. Baum, J. Singer, and S. Valins (eds.), *Advances in Environmental Psychology*, vol. 1. Hillsdale: Erlbaum, pp. 1–29.

Hartig, T.; Mang, M.; and Evans, G. W. (1991). "The restorative effects of natural environment experience." *Environment and Behavior* 23(1): 3–26.

Kaplan, S. (1978). "Attention and fascination: The search for cognitive clarity." In S. Kaplan and R. Kaplan (eds.), *Humanscape: Environments for people*. Belmont, CA: Duxbury. (Republished by Ulrich's, Ann Arbor, MI: 1982.)

Kaplan, S. (1983). "A model of person–environment compatibility." *Environment and Behavior* 15(3): 311–332.

Kaplan, S. (1987). "Mental fatigue and the designed environment." In J. Harvey and D. Henning (eds.), *Public environments*. Washington, DC: Environmental Design Research Association, pp. 55–60.

Kaplan, S. (1989). "Past environments and past stories in human effectiveness and well being." In G. Hardie, R. Moore, and H. Sanoff (eds.), *Changing paradigms*. Oklahoma City: Environmental Design Research Association, pp. 223–228.

Kaplan, S. (1992). "The restorative environment: Nature and human experience." In D. Relf (ed.), *The role of horticulture in human well-being and social development*. Portland, OR: Timber Press, pp. 134–142.

Kaplan, S. (1993). "The role of natural environment aesthetics in the restorative experience." In P. H. Gobster (ed.), *Managing urban and high-use recreation settings*. St. Paul, MN: USDA Forest Service, General Technical Report NC–163, pp. 46–49.

Kaplan, S. (1995). "The restorative benefits of nature: Toward an integrative framework." *Journal of Environmental Psychology* 15: 169–182.

Kaplan, S. (1995). "The urban forest as a source of psychological well-being." In G. A. Bradley (ed.), *Urban forest landscapes: Integrating multidisciplinary perspectives*. Seattle: University of Washington Press.

Kaplan, S., and Peterson, C. (1993). "Health and environment: A psychological analysis." *Landscape and Urban Planning* 26: 17–23.

Kaplan, S., and Talbot, J. F. (1983). "Psychological benefits of a wilderness experience." In I. Altman and J. F. Wohlwill (eds.), *Behavior and the natural environment*. New York: Plenum Press, pp. 163–203.

Mander, J. (1978). *Four arguments for the elimination of television*. New York: Morrow Quill.

Milgram, S. (1970). "The experience of living in cities." *Science* 167: 1461–1468.

Pigram, J. J. (1993). "Human-nature relationships: Leisure environments and natural settings." In T. Gärling and R. G. Golledge (eds.), *Behavior and environment: Psychological and geographical approaches*. Amsterdam: Elsevier Science Publishers.

Postman, N. (1985). *Amusing ourselves to death*. New York: Penguin Books.

Sharing Information

(also see chapter 10, "Engaging People")

Anderson, E. (1978). *Visual resource assessment: Local perceptions of familiar natural environments*. Unpublished doctoral dissertation, University of Michigan, Ann Arbor.

Bardwell, L. V. (1991). "Problem-framing: A perspective on environmental problem-solving." *Environmental Management* 15(5): 603–612.

Clarkson, J. D. (1970). "Ecology and spatial analysis." *Annals of the Association of American Geographers* 60: 700.

De Young, R., and Monroe, M. C. (1996). "Some fundamentals of engaging stories." *Environmental Education Research* 2: 171–179.

Dreyfus, H. L., and Dreyfus, S. E. (1984). "Mindless machines: Computers don't think like experts, and never will." *The Sciences* 24: 18–22.

Dwyer, J. F., and Hutchison, R. (1990). "Outdoor recreation participation and preferences by black and white Chicago households." In J. Vining (ed.), *Social science and natural resources management*. Boulder, CO: Westview Press.

Dwyer, J. F.; Hutchison, R.; and Wendling, R. C. (1981). "Participation of outdoor recreation by black and white Chicago households." Presented at the National Recreation and Park Association Symposium on Leisure Research, Minneapolis, October 26, 1981.

Fischhoff, B.; Lichtenstein, S.; Slovic, P.; Derby, S. L.; and Keeney, R. L. (1981). *Acceptable risk*. New York: Cambridge University Press. (See chapter 4: Professional judgment.)

Francis, M. (1987). "Urban open spaces." In E. H. Zube and G. T. Moore (eds.), *Advances in environment, behavior, and design*, vol. 1. New York: Plenum Press.

Franck, K. A., and Paxson, L. (1989). "Women and urban public space: Research, design, and policy issues." In I. Altman and E. H. Zube (eds.), *Public Places and Spaces*. New York: Plenum Press, pp. 121–146.

Fritschen, J. M., and Stynes, D. J. (1980). "Interpretation for urban audiences." In *Proceedings of the Association of Interpretative Naturalists Workshop*. Cape Cod, MA.

Gärling, T., and Golledge, R. G. (1989). "Environmental perception and cognition." In E. H. Zube and G. T. Moore (eds.), *Advances in environment, behavior, and design*. New York: Plenum Press.

Getz, D. A., and Kielbaso, J. J. (1982). "Inner city preference for trees and urban forestry programs." *Journal of Arboriculture* 8: 258–263.

Godbey, G., and Blaze, M. (1983). "Old people in urban parks." *Journal of Leisure Research* 15: 229–244.

Hammitt, W. E. (1978). *Visual and user preference for a bog environment*. Unpublished doctoral dissertation, University of Michigan, Ann Arbor.

Hammitt, W. E. (1979). "Measuring familiarity for natural environments through visual images." In *Proceedings of Our National Landscape Conference*. Berkeley, CA: USDA Forest Service, General Technical Report PSW–35, pp. 217–226.

Hammitt, W. E. (1981). "The familiarity-preference component of on-site recreational experiences." *Leisure Sciences* 4: 177–193.

Hester, R. T., Jr.; Blazej, N. J.; and Moore, I. S. (1996). "Whose wild? Resolving cultural and biological diversity conflicts in urban wilderness." Paper presented at Council of Educators in Landscape Architecture Annual Conference, Spokane, Washington, August 7–10, 1996.

Hudspeth, T. R. (1986). "Visual preference as a tool for facilitating citizen participation in urban waterfront revitalization." *Journal of Environmental Management* 23: 373–385.

Kaplan, R. (1990). "Collaboration from a cognitive perspective: Sharing models across expertise." In R. I. Selby, K. H. Anthony, J. Choi, and B. Orland (eds.), *Coming of age*. Oklahoma City: Environmental Design Research Association, pp. 45–51.

Kaplan, R. (1993). "Environmental appraisal, human needs, and a sustainable future." In T. Gärling and R. G. Golledge (eds.), *Behavior and environment: Psychological and geographical approaches*. Amsterdam: Elsevier Science Publishers, pp. 117–140.

Kaplan, R. (1995). "Informational issues: A perspective on human needs and inclinations." In G. A. Bradley (ed.), *Urban forest landscapes: Integrating multidisciplinary perspectives*. Seattle: University of Washington Press, pp. 60–71.

Kaplan, R., and Herbert, E. J. (1987). "Cultural and sub-cultural comparisons in preference for natural settings." *Landscape and Urban Planning* 14: 291–293.

Kaplan, R., and Herbert, E. J. (1988). "Familiarity and preference: A cross-cultural analysis." In J. L. Nasar (ed.), *Environmental aesthetics: Theory, research and application*. New York: Cambridge University Press, pp. 379–389.

Kaplan, R., and Kaplan S. (1989). "Variations and group differences." *The experience of nature*. New York: Cambridge University Press, pp. 72–116. (Republished by Ulrich's, Ann Arbor, MI: 1996.)

Kaplan, R., and Talbot, J. F. (1988). "Ethnicity and preference for natural settings: A review and recent findings." *Landscape and Urban Planning* 15: 107–117.

Kaplan, S. (1973). "Cognitive maps in perception and thought." In R. M. Downs and D. Stea (eds.), *Image and environment*. Chicago, IL: Aldine, pp. 63–78.

Kaplan, S. (1977). "Participation in the design process: A cognitive approach." In D. Stokols (ed.), *Perspectives on environment and behavior: Theory, research and application*. New York: Plenum Press, pp. 221–233.

Kaplan, S. (1991). "Beyond rationality: Clarity-based decision making." In T. Gärling and G. Evans (eds.), *Environment, cognition and action: An integrative multidisciplinary approach*. New York: Oxford University Press, pp. 171–190.

Kaplan, S., and Kaplan, R. (1982). "Problem solving and planning"; "Participation in environmental design and decision." *Cognition and environment: Functioning in an uncertain world.* New York: Praeger, pp. 146–173, 224–252. (Republished by Ulrich's, Ann Arbor, MI: 1989.)

Kearney, A. R. (1994). "Understanding global change: A cognitive perspective on communication through stories." *Climatic Change* 27: 419–441.

Kearney, A. R. (1997). "Expertise and cognitive clarity." *Some implications of cognitive map theory for environmental problem solving and decision making.* Unpublished doctoral dissertation, University of Michigan, Ann Arbor.

Kearney, A. R., and Kaplan, S. (1997). "Toward a methodology for the measurement of the knowledge structures of ordinary people: The conceptual content cognitive map (3CM)." *Environment and Behavior* 29: 579–617.

Metro, L. J.; Dwyer, J. F.; and Dreschler, E. S. (1981). *Forest experiences of fifth-grade Chicago public school students.* St. Paul, MN: USDA Forest Service, Research Paper NC–21.

Miller, P. A. (1984). *Visual preference and implications for coastal management: A perceptual study of the British Columbia shoreline.* Unpublished doctoral dissertation, University of Michigan, Ann Arbor.

Nassauer, J. I. (1995). "Culture and changing landscape structure." *Landscape Ecology* 10: 229–237.

Posner, M. I. (1973). *Cognition: An introduction.* Glenview, IL: Scott, Foresman.

Posner, M. I., and Keele, S. W. (1970). "Retention of abstract ideas." *Journal of Experimental Psychology* 83: 304.

Posner, M. I., and Rothbart, M. K. (1980). "The development of attentional mechanisms." In J. H. Flowers (ed.), *Nebraska symposium on motivation.* Lincoln: University of Nebraska Press.

Schroeder, H. W. (1982). "Preferred features of urban parks and forests." *Journal of Arboriculture* 8: 317–322.

Schroeder, H. W. (1983). "Variations in the perception of urban forest recreation sites." *Leisure Sciences* 5(3): 221–230.

Simmons, D. A. (1994). "Urban children's preferences for nature: Lessons for environmental education." *Children's Environments* 11: 194–203.

Talbot, J. F., and Kaplan, R. (1984). "Needs and fears: The response to trees and nature in the inner city." *Journal of Arboriculture* 10(8): 222–228.

Talbot, J. F., and Kaplan, R. (1993). "Preferences for nearby nature settings: Ethnic and age variations." In P. Gobster (ed.), *Managing urban and high-use recreation settings.* St. Paul, MN: USDA Forest Service, General Technical Report NC–163.

Vitz, P. C. (1990). "The use of stories in moral development: New psychological reasons for an old education method." *American Psychologist* 45: 709–720.

Wendling, R. C. (1980). "Black/white differences in outdoor recreation behavior: State-of-the-art and recommendations for management and research." *Social Research in National Parks and Wildlands Areas: Proceedings of the Conference.* Gatlinburg, Tennessee, March 21–22, 1980.

Yang, B. E., and Brown, T. J. (1992). "A cross-cultural comparison of preferences for landscape styles and landscape elements." *Environment and Behavior* 24: 471–507.

Yang, B. E., and Kaplan, R. (1990). "The perception of landscape style: A cross-cultural comparison." *Landscape and Urban Planning* 19: 251–262.

Yu, K. (1995). "Cultural variations in landscape preference: Comparisons among Chinese subgroups and Western design experts." *Landscape and Urban Planning* 32: 107–126.

Part II: Meeting the Challenges

Chapter 3: Fears and Preferences

Fears

Acredolo, L. P. (1982). "The familiarity factor in spatial research." *New Directions for Childhood Development* 15: 19–30.

Acredolo, L. P. (1990). "Behavioral approaches to spatial orientation in infancy." Conference of the National Institute of Mental Health. Catalogued in the *Annals of the New York Academy of Sciences* 608: 596–612.

Bixler, R.D.; Carlisle, C. L.; and Floyd, M. F. (1995). "Wayfinding aids: Getting the novice into the woods." *Legacy* 12: 25–29.

Bixler, R. D.; Carlisle, C. L.; Hammitt, W. E.; and Floyd, M. F. (1994). "Observed fears and discomforts among urban students on school field trips to wildland areas." *Journal of Environmental Education* 26: 24–33.

Bixler, R. D., and Floyd, M. F. (1997). "Nature is scary, disgusting and uncomfortable." *Environment and Behavior* 29(4): 443–467.

Bixler, R. D.; Floyd, M. F.; and Hammitt, W. E. (1995). "Feared stimuli are expected in specific situations: Using an expectancy approach and situationalism in self-report measures of fear." *Journal of Clinical Psychology* 51(4): 544–547.

Cantor, J., and Omdahl, B. L. (1991). "Effects of fictional media depictions of realistic threats on children's emotional responses, expectations, worries, and liking for related activities." *Communications Monograph* 58(4): 384–401.

Cooper-Marcus, C., and Sarkissian, W. (1986). *Housing as if people mattered: Site design guidelines for medium-density housing.* Berkeley: University of California Press, pp. 251–286.

Fisher, B. S., and Nasar, J. L. (1992). "Fear of crime in relation to three exterior site features: Prospect, refuge, and escape." *Environment and Behavior* 24: 35–65.

Gobster, P. H. (1991). "Forest vegetation in urban parks: Perceptions of inner city children." In G. A. Vander Stoep (ed.), *Proceedings of the 1991 Northeastern Recreation Research Symposium.* Chicago, IL: USDA Forest Service, General Technical Report NE–160, pp. 209–214.

Green Cities Initiative. (1994). *Healing America's cities: How urban parks can make cities safe and healthy.* San Francisco: Trust for Public Land.

Hammitt, W. E. (1978). *Visual and user preference for a bog environment.* Unpublished doctoral dissertation, University of Michigan, Ann Arbor.

Hammitt, W. E. (1979). "Measuring familiarity for natural environments through visual images." In *Proceedings of Our National Landscape Conference.* Berkeley, CA: USDA Forest Service, General Technical Report PSW–35, pp. 217–226.

Hammitt, W. E. (1981). "The familiarity-preference component of on-site recreational experiences." *Leisure Sciences* 4: 177–193.

Herzog, T. R., and Chernick, K. K. (in review). "Tranquillity and danger in urban and natural settings."

Hill, K. A. (1992). "Spatial competence of elderly hunters." *Environment and Behavior* 24: 779–794.

Kaplan, R. (1973). "Predictors of environmental preference: Designers and 'clients'." In W. F. E. Peiser (ed.), *Environmental design research.* Stroudsburg, PA: Dowden, Hutchinson, and Ross.

Kearney, A. R. (1996). "Public attitudes and preferences regarding the Indian River." Research report submitted to USDA Forest Service, North Central Forest Experiment Station, East Lansing, MI.

Kent, R. L., and Elliot, C. L. (1995). "Scenic routes linking and protecting natural and cultural landscape features: A greenway skeleton." *Landscape and Urban Planning* 33: 341–356.

Kuo, F. E.; Bacaicoa, M.; and Sullivan, W. C. (1998). "Transforming inner-city landscapes: Trees, sense of safety, and preference in urban public housing." *Environment and Behavior* 30(1): 28–59.

Lazarus, J., and Symonds, M. (1993). "Contrasting effects of protective and obstructive cover on avian vigilance." *Animal Behavior* 43: 519–521.

Lewis, C. A. (1978). "Nature city." In S. Kaplan and R. Kaplan (eds.), *Humanscape: Environments for people.* Belmont, CA: Duxbury, pp. 448–453. (Republished by Ulrich's, Ann Arbor, MI: 1982.)

Lieber, S. R., and Fesenmaier, D. R. (1985). "Physical and social conditions affecting recreational site preferences." *Environment and Planning A* 17: 1613–1625.

Martin, R. D. (1993). *Suburban residents' perception of wildlife habitat patches and corridors in their neighborhoods.* Unpublished thesis, University of Minnesota.

Metro, L. J.; Dwyer, J. F.; and Dreschler, E. S. (1981). *Forest experiences of fifth-grade Chicago public school students.* St. Paul, MN: USDA Forest Service, Research Paper NC–21.

Michael, S. E., and Hull IV, R. B. (1994). *The effects of vegetation on crime in urban parks.* Blacksburg, VA: Department of Forestry and Wildlife Resources, Virginia Polytechnic and State University.

Nager, A. R., and Wentworth, W.R. (1976). *Bryant Park: A comprehensive evaluation of its image and use with implications for urban open space design.* New York: Center for Human Environments, City University of New York.

Nasar, J. L. (1996). "Design in the context of fear: Increasing compatibility in difficult settings." In J. L. Nasar and B. B. Brown (eds.), *Public and private places: Proceedings of the twenty-seventh annual conference of the Environmental Design Research Association.* Edmund, OK: EDRA.

Nasar, J. L., and Fisher, B. (1993). "'Hot spots' of fear and crime: A multimethod investigation." *Journal of Environmental Psychology* 13: 187–206.

Nassauer, J. I. (1988a). "Landscape care: Perceptions of local people in landscape ecology and sustainable development." *Landscape and Land Use Planning.* 8: 27–41.

Nassauer, J. I. (1988b). "The aesthetics of horticulture: Neatness as a form of care." *Hortscience* 23: 973–977.

Nassauer, J. I. (1993). "Ecological function and the perception of suburban residential landscapes." In P. H. Gobster (ed.), *Managing urban and high use recreation settings.* St. Paul, MN: USDA Forest Service, General Technical Report NC–163.

Nassauer, J. I. (1995). "Messy ecosystems, orderly frames." *Landscape Journal.* 14(2): 161–170.

Newman, O. (1972). *Defensible space.* New York: Macmillan.

Newman, O. (1995). "Defensible space: A new physical planning tool for urban revitalization." *Journal of American Planning Association* 61(1): 149–155.

Perkins, D. D.; Wandersman, A. H.; Abraham, H.; Rich, R. C.; and Taylor, R. B. (1993). "The physical environment of street crime: Defensible space, territoriality, and incivilities." *Journal of Environmental Psychology* 13(1): 29–49.

Schroeder, H. W., and Anderson L. M. (1984). "Perception of personal safety in urban recreation sites." *Journal of Leisure Research* 16: 178–194.

Shaffer, G. S., and Anderson, L. M. (1985). "Perceptions of the security and attractiveness of urban parking lots." *Journal of Environmental Psychology* 5: 311–323.

Spotts, D. M., and Stynes, D. J. (1984). "Public awareness and knowledge of urban parks: A case study." *Journal of Park and Recreation Administration* 2: 1–12.

Spotts, D. M., and Stynes, D. J. (1985). "Measuring the public's familiarity with recreation areas." *Journal of Leisure Research* 17: 253–265.

Stewart, J., and McKenzie, R. L. (1978). "Composing urban spaces for security, privacy, and outlook." *Landscape Architecture* 68: 392–398.

Stoks, F. (1983). "Assessing urban environments for danger of violent crime: Especially rape." In D. Joiner, G. Brimilcombe, J. Daish, J. Gray, and D. Kernohan (eds.), *Proceedings of the Conference on People and Physical Environment Research.* Wellington, New Zealand: Ministry of Works and Development.

Talbot, J. F., and Kaplan, R. (1984). "Needs and fears: The response to trees and nature in the inner city." *Journal of Arboriculture* 10(8): 222–228.

Westover, T. N. (1985) "Perceptions of crime and safety in three midwestern parks." *Professional Geographer* 37(4): 410–420.

Westover, T. N. (1985). "Perceptions of rule compliance and law enforcement in urban and suburban parks." *Recreation Research Review* 12(2): 22–29.

Westover, T. N. (1986). "Park use and perception: Gender differences" *Journal of Park and Recreation Administration* 4(2): 1–8.

Wiedermann, D. (1985). "How secure are public open spaces?" *Garden and Landschaft* 95: 26–27.

Young, R. A., and Flowers, M. L. (1982). *Users of an urban natural area: Their characteristics, use patterns, satisfactions, and recommendations.* University of Illinois, Urbana-Champaign: Department of Forestry, Agricultural Experiment Station, Forestry research report 82–4.

Preferences
(also see Part I: By Way of Explanation)

Alexander, C.; Ishikawa S.; and Silverstein, M. (1977). "Pattern 121: Path shape." *A pattern language.* New York: Oxford University Press.

Aoki, Y.; Yasuoka, Y.; and Naito, M. (1985). "Assessing the impression of streetside greenery." *Landscape Research* 10: 9–13.

Balling, J. D., and Falk, J. H. (1982). "Development of visual preference for natural environments." *Environment and Behavior* 14: 5–28.

Bradley, G. A. (1996). *Forest aesthetics: Harvest practices in visually sensitive areas.* Olympia, WA: Washington Forest Protection Association.

Coeterier, J. F. (1983). "A photo validity test." *Journal of Environmental Psychology* 3: 315–323.

Cullen, G. (1971). *The concise townscape.* New York: Van Nostrand Reinhold.

Gimblett, R. H.; Itami, R. M.; and Fitzgibbon, J. E. (1985). "Mystery in an information processing model of landscape preference." *Landscape Journal* 4: 87–95.

Hammit, W. E. (1978). "A visual preference approach to measuring interpretive effectiveness." *Journal of Interpretation* 3(2): 33–37.

Hammitt, W. E. (1980). "Designing mystery into landscape-trail experiences." *Journal of Interpretation* 5(1): 16–19.

Herzog, T. R. (1984). "A cognitive analysis for field-and-forest environments." *Landscape Research* 9: 10–16.

Herzog, T. R. (1987). "A cognitive analysis of preference for natural environments: Mountains, canyons, and deserts." *Landscape Journal* 6: 140–152.

Herzog, T. R. (1989). "A cognitive analysis of preference for urban nature." *Journal of Environmental Psychology* 9: 27–43.

Herzog, T. R. (1992). "A cognitive analysis of preference for urban spaces." *Journal of Environmental Psychology* 12: 237–248.

Herzog, T. R., and Smith, G. A. (1988). "Danger, mystery, and environmental preference." *Environment and Behavior* 20: 320–344.

Hubbard, H. V., and Kimball, T. (1959). *An introduction to the study of landscape design.* New England: Cuneo Press, pp. 82–83.

Im, S. B. (1984). "Visual preferences in enclosed urban spaces." *Environment and Behavior* 16: 235–262.

Kaplan, R. (1984). "Dominant and variant values in environmental preference." In A. S. Devlin and S. L. Taylor (eds.), *Environmental preference and landscape preference.* New London: Connecticut College Press.

Kaplan, R. (1985). "The analysis of perception via preference: A strategy for studying how the environment is experienced." *Landscape Planning* 12: 161–176.

Kaplan, R., and Kaplan, S. (1989). "The prediction of preference." *The experience of nature.* New York: Cambridge Press, pp. 40–71. (Republished by Ulrich's, Ann Arbor, MI: 1996.)

Kaplan, R.; Kaplan, S.; and Brown, T. J. (1989). "Environmental preference: A comparison of four domains of predictors." *Environment and Behavior* 21: 509–530.

Kaplan, S. (1992). "Environmental preference in a knowledge-seeking knowledge-using organism." In J. H. Barkow, L. Cosmides, and J. Tooby (eds.), *The adapted mind.* New York: Oxford University Press, pp. 535–552.

Kaplan, S., and Kaplan, R. (1982). "Part two: Comprehension of the environment." *Cognition and environment: Functioning in an uncertain world.* New York: Praeger, pp. 11–70. (Republished by Ulrich's, Ann Arbor, MI: 1989.)

Kaplan, S.; Kaplan, R.; and Wendt, J. S. (1972). "Rated preference and complexity for natural and urban visual material." *Perception and Psychophysics* 12: 354–356.

Keane, T. D. (1990). *The role of familiarity in landscape aesthetics: A study of tallgrass prairie landscapes.* Unpublished doctoral dissertation, University of Michigan, Ann Arbor.

Nasar, J. L. (1987). "Environmental correlates of evaluative appraisals of central business district scenes." *Landscape and Urban Planning* 14: 117–130.

Nasar, J. L. (1989). "Perception, cognition, and evaluation of urban places." In I. Altman and E. H. Zube (eds.), *Public places and spaces.* New York: Plenum Press, pp. 31–56.

Schroeder, H. W. (1982). "Preferred features of urban parks and forests." *Journal of Arboriculture* 8: 317–322.

Schroeder, H. W. (1986). "Estimating park tree densities to maximize landscape esthetics." *Journal of Environmental Management* 23: 325–333.

Schroeder, H. W., and Anderson, L. M. (1984). "Perception of personal safety in urban recreation sites." *Journal of Leisure Research* 16: 178–194.

Schroeder, H. W., and Green, T. L. (1985). "Public preference for tree density in a municipal forest program." *Journal of Arboriculture* 11: 272–277.

Trent, R. B.; Neumann. E.; and Alon, K. (1986). "Presentation mode and question format artifacts in visual assessment research." *Landscape and Urban Planning* 14: 225–235.

Tyznik, A. (1981). "Trees as design elements in the landscape." *Journal of Arboriculture* 72: 53–55.

Ulrich, R. S. (1979). "Visual landscapes and psychological well-being." *Landscape Research* 4: 17–19.

Wecker, S. C. (1964). "Habitat selection" *Scientific American* 211 (4): 109–116.

Wohlwill, J. F. (1976). "Environmental aesthetics: The environment as a source of affect." In I. Altman and J. F. Wohlwill (eds.), *Human behavior and environment: Advances in theory and research,* vol. 1. New York: Plenum Press, pp. 37–86.

Wohlwill, J. F., and Harris, G. (1980). "Response to congruity or contrast for man-made features in natural recreation settings." *Leisure Sciences* 3(4): 349–365.

Woodcock, D. M. (1982). *A functionalist approach to environmental pre-ference*. Unpublished doctoral dissertation, University of Michigan, Ann Arbor.

Young, R. A., and Flowers, M. L. (1982). *Users of an urban natural area: Their characteristics, use patterns, satisfactions, and recommendations*. University of Illinois, Urbana-Champaign: Department of Forestry, Agricultural Experiment Station, Forestry research report 82–4.

Chapter 4: Way-finding

Allen, G. L., and Kirasic, K. C. (1985). "Effects of the cognitive organization of route knowledge on judgment of macrospatial distance." *Memory and Cognition* 13: 218–227.

Appleyard, D. (1978). "Styles and methods of structuring a city." In S. Kaplan and R. Kaplan (eds.), *Humanscape: Environments for people*. Belmont, CA: Duxbury. (Republished by Ulrich's, Ann Arbor, MI: 1982.)

Arthur, P., and Passini, R. (1992). *Wayfinding: People, signs and architecture*. New York: McGraw-Hill.

Bixler, R. D.; Carlisle, C. L.; and Floyd, M. F. (1995). "Wayfinding aids: Getting the novice into the woods." *Legacy* 12: 25–29.

Bixler, R. D.; Carlisle, C. L.; Hammitt, W. E.; and Floyd, M. F. (1994). "Observed fears and discomforts among urban students on school field trips to wildland areas." *Journal of Environmental Education* 26: 24–33.

Bixler, R. D.; Floyd, M. F.; and Hammitt, W. E. (1995). "Feared stimuli are expected in specific situations: Using an expectancy approach and situationalism in self-report measures of fear." *Journal of Clinical Psychology* 51(4): 544–547.

Blades, M. (1991). "Wayfinding theory and research: The need for a new approach." In D.M. Mark and A. U. Frank (eds.), *Cognitive and linguistic aspects of geographic science*. Dordrecht, Netherlands: Kluwer Academic Publishers, pp. 137–165.

Bluestein, N., and Acredolo, L. (1979). "Developmental changes in map-reading skills." *Child Development* 50: 691–697.

Cornell, E. H.; Heth, C. D.; and Broda, L. S. (1989). "Children's wayfinding: Response to instructions to use environmental landmarks." *Developmental Psychology* 25(5): 755–764.

Devlin, A. S., and Bernstein, J. (1995). "Interactive wayfinding: Uses of cues by men and women." *Journal of Environmental Psychology* 15(1): 23–28.

Falk, J. H., and Dierking, L. D. (1992). *The museum experience*. Washington, DC: Whalesback Books.

Forrest, D., and Castner, H. W. (1985). "Design and perception of point symbols for tourist maps." *Cartographic Journal* 22: 11–19.

Gärling, T.; Lindberg, E.; Carreriras, M.; and Böök, A. (1986). "Reference systems in cognitive maps." *Journal of Environmental Psychology* 6: 1–18.

Gluck, M. (1991). "Making sense of human wayfinding: Review of cognitive and linguistic knowledge for personal navigation with a new research direction." In D. M. Mark and A. U. Frank (eds.), *Cognitive and linguistic aspects of geographic space*. Dordrecht, Netherlands: Kluwer Academic Publishers, pp. 117–135.

Golledge, R. G. (1991). "Environmental cognition." In D. Stokols and I. Altman (eds.), *Handbook of environmental psychology*, vol. 1. Malabar, FL: Krieger, pp. 131–174.

Golledge, R. G. (1993). "Geographical perspectives on spatial cognition." In T. Gärling and R. G. Golledge (eds.), *Behavior and environment: Psychological and geographical approaches*. Amsterdam: Elsevier Science Publishers, pp. 16–46.

Kaplan, R. (1976). "Way-finding in the natural environment." In G. T. Moore and R. G. Golledge (eds.), *Environmental knowing: Theories, perspectives, and methods*. Stroudsburg, PA: Dowden, Hutchinson, and Ross.

Kirasic, K. C., and Mathes, E. A. (1990). "Effects of different means for conveying environmental information on elderly adults' spatial cognition and behavior." *Environment and Behavior* 22: 591–607.

Kuo, F. E. (1995). *Facilitating learning and adaptation in unfamiliar environments: Maps, spatial orientation, and the university*. Unpublished doctoral dissertation, University of Michigan, Ann Arbor.

Levine, M. (1982). "You are here maps: Psychological considerations." *Environment and Behavior* 14(2): 221–237.

Levine, M.; Marchan, I.; and Hanley, G. (1984). "Placement and misplacement of you-are-here maps." *Environment and Behavior* 16(2): 139–157.

Loomis, R. (1987). *Visitor evaluation*. Nashville, TN: American Association for State and Local History.

Lynch, K. (1960). *The image of the city*. Cambridge, MA: MIT Press.

Lynch, K. (1984). *Site planning*, 3rd edition. Cambridge, MA: MIT Press.

Mackay-Yarnal, C. M., and Coulson, M. R. C. (1982). "Recreational map design and map use: An experiment." *Cartographic Journal* 19(1): 16–27.

Mandler, G. (1975). "Consciousness: Respectful, useful, and probably necessary." In R. L. Solso (ed.), *Information processing and cognitive psychology*. Hillsdale, NJ: Erlbaum.

Mandler, G. (1975). "Memory storage and retrieval: Some limits on the research of attention and consciousness." In P. M. Rabbitt and S. Dornic (eds.), *Attention and performance*, vol. 5. London: Academic Press.

Monmonier, M. S. (1996). *How to lie with maps*. Chicago: University of Illinois Press.

Montello, D. R. (1991). "Spatial orientation and angularity of urban routes: A field study." *Environment and Behavior* 23: 47–69.

O'Neill, M. J. (1991). "Effects of signage and floor plan configuration on wayfinding accuracy." *Environment and Behavior* 23: 553–574.

Talbot, J. F.; Kaplan, R.; Kuo, F. E.; and Kaplan, S. (1993). "Factors that enhance effectiveness of visitor maps." *Environment and Behavior* 25: 743–760.

Warren, D. H. (1994). "Self-localization on plan and oblique maps." *Environment and Behavior* 26: 71–98.

Warren, D. H., and Scott, T. E. (1993). "Map alignment in traveling multi-segment routes." *Environment and Behavior* 25: 643–666.

Weisman, J. (1981). "Evaluating architectural legibility: Way-finding in the built environment." *Environment and Behavior* 13(2): 189–204.

Wohlwill, J. F., and Harris, G. (1980). "Response to congruity or contrast for man-made features in natural recreation settings." *Leisure Sciences* 3(4): 349–365.

Chapter 5: Restorative Environments

(also see "The Psychological Costs of Managing Information," in chapter 2)

Alexander, C.; Ishikawa S.; and Silverstein, M. (1977). "Pattern 176: Garden seat." *A pattern language*. New York: Oxford University Press.

Anderson, L. M.; Mulligan, B. E.; Goodman, L. S.; and Regen, H. Z. (1983). "Effects of sounds on preferences for outdoor settings." *Environment and Behavior* 15(5): 539–566.

Aoki, Y.; Yasuoka, Y.; and Naito, M. (1985). "Assessing the impression of streetside greenery." *Landscape Research* 10: 9–13.

Canin, L. H. (1992). *Psychological restoration among AIDS caregivers: Maintaining self-care*. Unpublished doctoral dissertation, University of Michigan, Ann Arbor.

Chenney, T.; Hofmockel, M.; and Ryan, R. (1985). *Japanese gardens: Traditions in design*. Unpublished Senior Project Report, Landscape Architecture Department, California Polytechnic State University, San Luis Obispo, CA.

Cimprich, B. E. (1990). *Attentional fatigue and restoration in individuals with cancer*. Unpublished doctoral dissertation, University of Michigan, Ann Arbor.

Cimprich, B. E. (1992). "Attentional fatigue following breast cancer surgery." *Nursing and Health* 15(3): 199–207.

Cooper-Marcus, C., and Sarkissian, W. (1986). *Housing as if people mattered: Site design guidelines for medium-density housing*. Berkeley: University of California Press, p. 47.

Devlin, A. S.; Morton, J.; Zaff, J.; Freedland, C.; and Mendez, N. (1996). "Dormitory environments, daily stress, and environmental preference." In J. L Nasar and B. B. Brown (eds.), *Public and private places: Proceedings of the twenty-seventh annual conference of the Environmental Design Research Association*. Edmund, OK: EDRA, pp. 98–105.

Francis, M. (1995). *The healing dimensions of people–plant relations: A research symposium*. Davis: University of California Center for Design Research.

Francis, M., and Hester, R. T., Jr. (1990). *The meaning of gardens*. Cambridge, MA: MIT Press.

Frewald, D. B. (1989). *Preferences for older buildings: A psychological approach to architectural design*. Unpublished doctoral dissertation, University of Michigan, Ann Arbor.

Godbey, G., and Blazey, M. (1983). "Old people in urban parks." *Journal of Leisure Research* 15: 229–244.

Harrison, C.; Limb, M.; and Burgess, J. (1987). "Nature in the city: Popular values for a living world." *Journal of Environmental Management* 25: 347–362.

Hartig, T. (1993). "Testing restorative environments theory." *Dissertation Abstracts International* 54, 08B. (University Microfilms No. 94–02, 422.)

Hartig, T.; Böök, A.; Garvill, J.; Olsson, T.; and Gärling, T. (1996). "Environmental influences on psychological restoration." *Scandinavian Journal of Psychology* 37: 378–393.

Hartig, T.; Mang, M.; and Evans, G. W. (1991). "The restorative effects of natural environment experience." *Environment and Behavior* 23(1): 3–26.

Heerwagen, J. H., and Orians, G. H. (1986). "Adaptations to windowlessness: A study of the use of visual decor in windowed and windowless offices." *Environment and Behavior* 18: 623–639.

Herzog, T. R.; Black, A. M.; Fountaine, K. A.; and Knotts, D. J. (1997). "Reflection and attentional recovery as distinctive benefits of restorative environments." *Journal of Environmental Psychology* 17: 165–170.

Herzog, T.R., and Bosley, P. J. (1992). "Tranquillity and preference as affective qualities of natural environments." *Journal of Environmental Psychology* 12: 115–127.

Herzog, T. R., and Gale, T. A. (1996). "Preference for urban buildings as a function of age and nature context." *Environment and Behavior* 28: 44–72.

Ito, T. (1973). *Space and illusion in a Japanese garden.* New York: Weatherhill Press.

Kaplan, R. (1973). "Some psychological benefits of gardening." *Environment and Behavior* 5: 145–161.

Kaplan, R. (1985). Nature at the doorstep: Residential satisfaction and the nearby environment." *Journal of Architectural and Planning Research* 2: 115–127.

Kaplan, R. (1993). "The role of nature in the context of the workplace." *Landscape and Urban Planning* 26: 193–201.

Kaplan, S. (1989). "Past environments and past stories in human effectiveness and well being." In G. Hardie, R. Moore, and H. Sanoff (eds.), *Changing paradigms.* Oklahoma City: Environmental Design Research Association, pp. 223–228.

Korpela, K., and Hartig, T. (1996). "Restorative qualities of favorite places." *Journal of Environmental Psychology* 16: 221–233.

McIntyre, N.; Cuskelly, G.; and Auld, C. (1991). "The benefits of urban parks." *Australian Parks and Recreation* 27: 11–18.

Moore, E. O. (1981). "A prison environment's effect on health care service demands." *Journal of Environmental Systems* 11: 17–34.

Relf, D. (1992). "Human issues in horticulture." *Hort Technology* 2(2): 159–171.

Relf, D. (1992). *The role of horticulture in human well-being and social development: A national symposium.* Portland, OR: Timber Press.

Sadalla, E. K., and Staplin, L. J. (1980). "An information model for distance cognition." *Environment and Behavior* 12: 183–193.

Shaw, W. W.; Mangun, W. R.; and Lyons, J. R. (1985). "Residential enjoyment of wildlife resources by Americans." *Leisure Sciences* 7: 361–375.

Stankey, G. H. (1989). "Solitude for the multitudes." In I. Altman and E. H. Zube (eds.), *Public places and spaces.* New York: Plenum Press, pp. 277–299.

Talbot, J. F. (1988). "Planning concerns relating to urban nature settings: The role of size and other physical features." In Nasar, J. L. (ed.), *Environmental aesthetics: Theory, research, and applications.* Cambridge: Cambridge University Press.

Talbot, J. F., and Bardwell, L. V. (1989). "Making 'open spaces' that work: Research and guidelines for natural areas in medium-density housing." In G. Hardie, R. Moore, and H. Sanoff (eds.), *Changing paradigms.* Oklahoma City: Environmental Design Research Association, pp. 110–115.

Talbot, J. F., and Kaplan, R. (1986). "Judging the sizes of urban open areas: Is bigger always better?" *Landscape Journal* 5: 83–92.

Tennessen, C. M., and Cimprich, B. E. (1995). "Views to nature: Affects of attention." *Journal of Environmental Psychology* 15(1): 77–85.

Ulrich, R. S. (1979). "Visual landscapes and psychological well-being." *Landscape Research* 4: 17–19.

Ulrich, R. S. (1984). "View through a window may influence recovery from surgery." *Science* 224: 420–421.

Ulrich, R. S.; Lunden, O.; and Eltinge, J. L. (1996). "Effects of viewing nature and abstract pictures on heart surgery patients." In J. L. Nasar and B. B. Brown (eds.), *Public and private places: Proceedings of the twenty-seventh annual conference of the Environmental Design Research Association.* Edmund, OK: EDRA

Ulrich, R. S., and Simmons, R. F. (1986). "Recovery from stress during exposure to everyday outdoor environments." In *Proceedings of EDRA 17.* Washington, DC: Environmental Design and Research Association.

Verderber, S. (1982). "Designing for the therapeutic functions of windows in the hospital environment." In P. Bart, et al. (eds.), *Knowledge in design.* Washington DC: Environmental Design Research Association, pp. 476–492.

Verderber, S. (1986). "Dimensions of person-window transactions in the hospital environment." *Environment and Behavior* 18: 450–466.

Verderber, S., and Reuman, D. (1987). "Windows, views, and health status in hospital therapeutic environments." *Journal of Architectural and Planning Research* 4: 120–133.

West, M. J. (1986). *Landscape views and stress responses in the prison environment.* Unpublished master's thesis, University of Washington, Seattle.

Young, R. A., and Flowers, M. L. (1982). *Users of an urban natural area: Their characteristics, use patterns, satisfactions, and recommendations.* University of Illinois, Urbana-Champaign: Department of Forestry, Agricultural Experiment Station, Forestry research report 82-4.

Part III: Design and Management Opportunities

Chapter 6: Gateways and Partitions

Alexander, C.; Ishikawa S.; and Silverstein, M. (1977). "Pattern 112: Entrance transition." *A pattern language.* New York: Oxford University Press.

Cooper-Marcus, C., and Sarkissian, W. (1986). *Housing as if people mattered: Site design guidelines for medium-density housing.* Berkeley: University of California Press, p. 74.

Chapter 7: Trails and Locomotion

Alexander, C.; Ishikawa S.; and Silverstein, M. (1977). "Pattern 120: Paths and goals"; "Pattern 241: Seat spots." *A pattern language.* New York: Oxford University Press.

Allton, D. J., and Lieber, S. R. (1983). "Attributes of Chicago trail areas." *Leisure Science* 5(3): 197–220.

Axelsson-Lindgren, C., and Sorte, G. (1987). "Public response to differences between visually distinguishable forest stands in a recreation area." *Landscape and Urban Planning* 14: 211–217.

Cooper-Marcus, C., and Sarkissian, W. (1986). *Housing as if people mattered: Site design guidelines for medium-density housing.* Berkeley: University of California Press, pp. 238–240.

Field, D. R., and Wagar, J. A. (1976). "People and interpretation." In G. Sharpe (ed.), *Interpreting the environment.* New York: John Wiley, pp. 43–56.

Flink, C., and Searns, R. M. (1993). *Greenways: A guide to planning, design, and development.* Washington, DC: Island Press.

Gobster, P. H. (1991). "Urban park trail use: An observational approach." In G. A. Vander Stoep (ed.), *Proceedings of the 1991 Northeastern Recreation Research Symposium.* Chicago, IL: USDA Forest Service, General Technical Report NE–160, pp. 215–221.

Gobster, P. H. (1995). "Perceptions and use of a metropolitan greenway system for recreation." *Landscape and Urban Planning* 33: 401–413.

Hammitt, W. E., and Cherem, G. J. (1980). "Photographic perceptions as an on-site tool for designing forest trails." *Southern Journal of Applied Forestry* 4(2): 94–97.

Hendee, J. C., and Schoenfield. C. (1973). *Human dimensions in wildlife programs.* Rockville, MD: Mercury Press.

Keyes, B. E., and Hammitt W. E. (1984). "Visitor reaction to interpretive signs on a destination-oriented forest trail." *Journal of Interpretation* 9(1): 11–17.

Kroh, D., and Gimblett, R. H. (1992). "Comparing live experience with pictures in articulating landscape preference." *Landscape Research* 17(2): 58–69.

Lieber, S. R., and Allton, D. J. (1983). "Modeling trail area evaluations in metropolitan Chicago." *Journal of Leisure Research* 15(3): 184–202.

Lieber, S. R, and Fesenmaier, D. R. (1985). "Physical and social conditions affecting recreational site preferences." *Environment and Planning A* 17: 1613–1625.

Little, C. E. (1990). *Greenways for America*. Baltimore, MD: Johns Hopkins University Press.

Louviere, J. J.; Anderson, D. A.; and Louviere, C. H. (1991). *Bike trail choice among Chicago area trail users*. North Central Forest Experiment Stations, Chicago, IL: USDA Forest Service, unpublished final report.

Mertes, J. D., and Hall, J. R. (1995). *Park, recreation, open space and greenway guidelines*. Arlington, VA: National Recreation and Park Association.

Passini, R. (1987). "Brain lesions and their effect on wayfinding: A review." In J. Harvey and D. Henning (eds.) *Public environments*. Washington, DC: Environmental Design Research Association, pp. 61–67.

Ryan, K. L., ed. (1993). *Trails for the twenty-first century: Planning, design, and management manual for multi-use trails*. Washington, DC: Island Press.

Talbot, J. F. (1993). "Public participation in rail-trail planning: Two case studies." In P. H. Gobster (ed.), *Managing urban and high use recreation settings*. St. Paul, MN: USDA Forest Service, General Technical Report NC–163.

Westphal, L. M., and Lieber, S. R. (1986). "Predicting the effect of alternative trail design on visitor satisfaction in park settings." *Landscape Journal* 5(1): 39–44.

Wiberg-Carlson, D., and Schroeder, H. W. (1992). *Modeling and mapping urban bicyclists preferences for trail environments*. St. Paul, MN: USDA Forest Service, Research Paper NC–303.

Chapter 8: Views and Vistas

(also see part I, "By Way of Explanation," and in part II, chapter 3, "Fears and Preferences," and chapter 5, "Restorative Environments")

Alexander, C.; Ishikawa S.; and Silverstein, M. (1977). "Pattern 62: High places"; Pattern 134: Zen view." *A pattern language*. New York: Oxford University Press.

Appleton, J. (1975). *The experience of landscape*. London: John Wiley.

Appleton, J. (1984). "Prospects and refuges re-visited." *Landscape Journal* 3: 91–103.

Hammitt, W. E. (1988). "Visual and management preferences of sightseers." In F. P. Noe and W. E. Hammitt (eds.), *Visual preferences along the Blue Ridge Parkway*. Washington, DC: U.S. Department of Interior, National Park Service, pp. 11–36.

Hammitt, W. E.; Patterson, M. E.; and Noe, F. P. (1994). "Identifying and predicting visual preference of Southern Appalachian Forest recreation vistas." *Journal of Landscape and Urban Planning* 29: 171–183.

Ito, T. (1973). *Space and illusion in a Japanese garden*. New York: Weatherhill Press.

Chapter 9: Places and Their Elements

Alexander, C.; Ishikawa S.; and Silverstein, M. (1977). "Pattern 64: Pools and streams"; "Pattern 71: Still water"; "Pattern 114: Hierarchy of open space";

"Pattern 163: Outdoor room"; "Pattern 171: Tree places"; and "Pattern 173: Garden wall." *A pattern language.* New York: Oxford University Press.

Chenoweth, R. E., and Gobster, P. H. (1990). "The nature and ecology of aesthetic experiences in the landscape." *Landscape Journal* 9: 1–8.

Coley, R. L.; Kuo, F. E.; and Sullivan, W.C. (1997). "Where does community grow? The social context created by nature in urban public housing." *Environment and Behavior* 29(4): 468–494.

Dwyer, J. F.; Schroeder, H. W.; and Gobster, P. H. (1991). "The significance of urban trees and forests: Toward a deeper understanding of values." *Journal of Arboriculture* 17(10): 276–284.

Dwyer, J. F.; Schroeder, H. W.; and Gobster, P. H. (1994). "The deep significance of urban trees and forests." In R. H. Platt, R. A. Rowntree, and P. C. Muick (eds.), *Preserving and restoring biodiversity.* Amherst: University of Massachusetts Press, pp. 137–150.

Ellsworth, J. C. (1982). *Visual assessment of rivers and marshes: An examination of the relationship of visual units, perceptual variables, and preference.* Unpublished master's thesis, Utah State University, Logan.

Getz, D. A., and Kielbaso, J. J. (1982). "Inner city preference for trees and urban forestry programs." *Journal of Arboriculture* 8: 258–263.

Hart, R. (1979). *Children's experience of place.* New York: Irvington Publishers.

Herzog, T. R. (1985). "A cognitive analysis of preference for waterscapes." *Journal of Environmental Psychology* 5: 225–241.

Kaplan, R. (1977). "Preference and everyday nature: Method and application." In D. Stokols (ed.), *Perspectives on environment and behavior: Theory, research, and applications.* New York: Plenum Press.

Kirkby, M. (1989). "Nature as a refuge in children's environments." *Children's Environments Quarterly* 6(1): 7–12.

Kuo, F. E.; Bacaicoa, M.; and Sullivan, W. C. (1997). "Transforming inner-city landscapes: Trees, sense of safety, and preference in urban public housing." *Environment and Behavior* 30(1): 28–59.

Levin, J. (1977). *Riverside preference: On-site and photographic reactions.* Unpublished master's thesis, University of Michigan, Ann Arbor.

Lynch, K. (1977). *Growing up in cities: Studies of the spatial environments of adolescence in Cracow, Melbourne, Mexico City, Salta, Toluca, and Warszawa.* Cambridge, MA: MIT Press.

Moore, R. C. (1986). *Childhood domain: Play and place in child development.* London: Croom Helm.

Newman, O. (1972). *Defensible space.* New York: Macmillan.

Newman, O. (1995). "Defensible space: A new physical planning tool for urban revitalization." *Journal of American Planning Association* 61(1): 149–155.

Owens, P. E. (1988). "Natural landscapes, gathering places and prospect refuge: Characteristics of outdoor places valued by teens." *Children's Environments Quarterly* 5: 17–24.

Ruddell, E. J., and Hammitt, W. E. (1987). "Prospect refuge theory: A psychological orientation for edge effect in recreation environments." *Journal of Leisure Research* 19(4): 249–260.

Ryan, R. L. (1995). *Perceptual river corridors: Understanding environmental preference in America's countryside.* Unpublished master's thesis, University of Michigan, Ann Arbor.

Schroeder, H. W. (1988). "The experience of significant landscapes at Morton Arboretum." *Proceedings of the 1987 Society of American Foresters National Convention,* Minneapolis, October 18–21, 1987, pp. 378–381.

Schroeder, H.W.; Buhyoff, G. J.; and Cannon, W. N., Jr. (1986). "Cross-validation of predictive models for aesthetic quality of residential streets." *Journal of Environmental Management* 23: 309–316.

Schroeder, H. W., and Cannon, W. N., Jr. (1983). "The aesthetic contribution of trees to residential streets in Ohio towns." *Journal of Arboriculture* 9: 237–243.

Schroeder, H. W., and Ruffolo, S. R. (1996). "Householder evaluations of street trees in a Chicago suburb." *Journal of Arboriculture* 22(1): 35–43.

Sheets, V. L., and Manzer, C. D. (1991). "Affect, cognition, and urban vegetation: Some effects of adding trees along city streets." *Environment and Behavior* 23: 285–304.

Sullivan, W. C., and Kuo, F. E. (1996). *Do trees strengthen urban communities, reduce domestic violence?* Atlanta, GA: USDA Forest Service, Forestry Report no. R8–FR 56.

Talbot, J., and Frost, J. L. (1989). "Magical playscapes." *Childhood Education* 66: 11–19.

Talbot, J. F. (1982). "Zoning reconsidered: The impacts of environmental aesthetics in urban neighborhoods." In P. Bart, A. Chen, and G. Francescato (eds.), *Proceedings of EDRA 13: Knowledge for Design.* Washington, DC: Environmental Design and Research Association.

Talbot, J. F.; Bardwell, L. V.; and Kaplan, R. (1987). "The functions of urban nature: Uses and values of different types of urban nature settings." *Journal of Architecture and Planning Research* 4: 47–63.

Talbot, J. F., and Kaplan. R. (1986). "Judging the sizes of urban open areas: Is bigger always better?" *Landscape Journal* 5: 83–92.

Taylor, A. F.; Wiley, A.; Kuo, F. E.; and Sullivan, W. C. (1998). "Growing up in the inner city: Green spaces as places to grow." *Environment and Behavior* 30(1): 3–27.

Wolf, K. L. (1993). *Shoreline residential development: Landscape management alternatives and public preference.* Unpublished doctoral dissertation, University of Michigan, Ann Arbor.

Yang, B. E. (1988). *A cross-cultural comparison for Korean, Japanese, and western landscape styles.* Unpublished doctoral dissertation, University of Michigan, Ann Arbor.

Yang, B. E., and Brown, T. J. (1992). "A cross-cultural comparison of preferences for landscape styles and landscape elements." *Environment and Behavior* 24: 471–507.

Yang, B. E., and Kaplan, R. (1990). "The perception of landscape style: A cross-cultural comparison." *Landscape and Urban Planning* 19: 251–262.

Zube, E. H. (1978). "The natural history of urban trees." In S. Kaplan and R.

Kaplan (eds.), *Humanscape: Environments for people*. Belmont, CA: Duxbury. (Republished by Ulrich's, Ann Arbor, MI: 1982.)

Part IV: With People in Mind

Chapter 10: Engaging People
(also see chapter 2, "Sharing Information")

Ames, R. G. (1980). "Urban tree planting programs: A sociological perspective." *Hortscience* 15(2): 135–137.

Anderson, E. (1978). *Visual resource assessment: Local perceptions of familiar natural environments*. Unpublished doctoral dissertation, University of Michigan, Ann Arbor.

Anderson, L. M., and Schroeder, H. W. (1983). "Application of wildland scenic assessment methods to the urban landscape." *Landscape Planning* 10: 219–237.

Bardwell, L. V. (1991). "Success stories: Imagery by example." *Journal of Environmental Education* 23(1): 5–10.

Bardwell, L. V. (1996). "The human face of environmental problem solving: Insights for environmental success stories." In J. L. Nasar and B. B. Brown (eds.), *Public and private places: Proceedings of the twenty-seventh annual conference of the Environmental Design Research Association*. Edmund, OK: EDRA, pp. 144–150.

Bassett, T. J. (1979). "Reaping on the margins: A century of community gardening in America." *Landscape* 25: 1–8.

Bradley, G. A. (1996). "Small experiments for the protection of the scenic resource." In J. L. Nasar, and B. B. Brown (eds.), *Public and private places: Proceedings of the twenty-seventh annual conference of the Environmental Design Research Association*. Edmund, OK: EDRA.

Brower, S. (1977). *The design of neighborhood parks*. Baltimore: City Planning Commission.

Brower, S.; Dockett, K.; and Taylor, R. (1983). "Residents' perceptions of territorial features and perceived local threat." *Environment and Behavior* 15: 419–426.

Brower, S. N. (1988). *Design in familiar places: What makes home environments look good*. New York: Praeger.

Carr, S.; Francis, M.; Rivlin, L. G.; and Stone, A. M. (1992). *Public space*. Cambridge: Cambridge University Press.

Chavis, D. M.; Stucky, P. E.; and Wandersman, A. (1983). "Returning basic research to the community: A relationship between scientist and citizen." *American Psychologist* 38(4): 424–434.

Cundiff, B. (1996). "Invasion of primacy." *Nature Canada* 25(2): 32–37.

Deardorff, H. (1996). "Redesigning the small town mainstreet: Participation, small experiments and unique solutions." In J. L. Nasar and B. B. Brown (eds.), *Public and private places: Proceedings of the twenty-seventh annual conference of the Environmental Design Research Association.* Edmund, OK: EDRA.

Dravnieks, G., and Pitcher, P. C. (1982). *Public participation in resource planning: Selected literature abstracts.* Berkeley, CA: United States Department of Agriculture, Forest Service.

Florin, P., and Wandersman, A. (1990). "An introduction to citizen participation, voluntary organizations, and community development: Insights for empowerment through research." *American Journal of Community Psychology* 18(1): 41–54.

Fox, T.; Koeppel, I.; and Kellam, S. (1985). *Struggle for space: The greening of New York City, 1970–1984.* New York: Neighborhood Open Space Coalition.

Francis, M. (1987). "The making of democratic streets." In A. Vernez-Moudon (ed.), *Streets are public.* New York: Van Nostrand Reinhold.

Francis, M. (1987). "Urban open spaces." In E. H. Zube and G. T. Moore (eds.), *Advances in environment, behavior, and design*, vol. 1. New York: Plenum Press.

Francis, M. (1988). "Negotiating between children and adult design values in open space projects." *Design Studies* 9(2): 187–195.

Francis, M. (1989). "Control as a dimension of public-space quality." In I. Altman and E. H. Zube (eds.), *Public places and spaces.* New York: Plenum Press, pp. 147–169.

Francis, M.; Cashdan, L.; and Paxson, L. (1984). *Community open spaces.* Washington, DC: Island Press.

Fried, M. (1963). "Grieving for a lost home." In L. J. Duhl (ed.) *The urban condition: People and policy in the metropolis.* New York: Basic Books.

Gobster, P. H. (1997). "The Chicago wilderness and its critics. Part III, the other side: A survey of arguments." *Restoration and Management Notes* 15(1): 32–37.

Gold, S. M. (1972). "Nonuse of neighborhood parks." *Journal of the American Institute of Planners* 38: 369–378.

Grove, Morgan. (1993). "The urban resources initiative: Community benefits from forestry." In P. H. Gobster (ed.), *Managing urban and high-use recreation settings.* St. Paul, MN: USDA Forest Service, General Technical Report NC–163, pp. 46–49.

Gundry, K. G., and Heberlein, T. A. (1984). *Do public meetings represent the public?* Madison: University of Wisconsin, Rural Sociology Department.

Hammitt, W. E. (1988). "Visual and management preferences of sightseers." In F. P. Noe and W. E. Hammitt (eds.), *Visual preferences along the Blue Ridge Parkway.* Washington, DC: U.S. Department of Interior, National Park Service, pp. 11–36.

Hayward, J. (1989). "Urban Parks: Research, planning, and social change." In I. Altman and E. H. Zube (eds.), *Public places and spaces.* New York: Plenum Press, pp. 193–216.

Hester, R. T., Jr. (1984). *Planning neighborhood space with people.* New York: Van Nostrand Reinhold.

Hester, R. T., Jr. (1990). *Community design primer.* Mendocino, CA: Ridge Times Press.

Hester, R. T., Jr. (1995). "Life, liberty and the pursuit of sustainable happiness." *Places* 9(3): 2–17.

Hester, R. T., Jr. (1996). "Wanted: Local participation with a view." In J. L. Nasar and B. B. Brown (eds.), *Public and private places: Proceedings of the twenty-seventh annual conference of the Environmental Design Research Association.* Edmund, OK: EDRA, pp. 42–52.

Hitchmough, J. (1993). "The urban bush." *Landscape Design* 222: 13–17.

Kaplan, R. (1977). "Preference and everyday nature: Method and application." In D. Stokols (ed.), *Perspectives on environment and behavior: Theory, research, and applications.* New York: Plenum Press.

Kaplan, R. (1978). "Participation in environmental design: Some considerations and a case study." In S. Kaplan and R. Kaplan (eds.), *Humanscape: Environments for people.* Belmont, CA: Duxbury. (Republished by Ulrich's, Ann Arbor, MI: 1982.)

Kaplan, R. (1980). "Citizen participation in the design and evaluation of a park." *Environment and Behavior* 12: 494–507.

Kaplan, R. (1984). "Assessing human concerns for environment decision-making." In S. L. Hart, G.A. Enk, and W. F. Hornick (eds.), *Improving impact assessment: Increasing the relevance and utilization of technical and scientific information.* Boulder, CO: Westview Press, pp. 37–56.

Kaplan, R. (1987). "Simulation models and participation: Designers and 'clients'." In J. Harvey and D. Henning (eds.), *Public environments.* Washington, DC: Proceedings of the Environmental Design Research Association, pp. 96–102.

Kaplan, R. (1993). "Physical models in decision making for design: Theoretical and methodological issues." In R. W. Marans and D. Stokols (eds.), *Environmental simulation: Research and policy issues.* New York: Plenum Press.

Kaplan, R. (1996). "The small experiment: Achieving more with less." In J. L. Nasar and B. B. Brown (eds.), *Public and private places: Proceedings of the twenty-seventh annual conference of the Environmental Design Research Association.* Edmund, OK: EDRA, pp. 170–174.

Kaplan, S. (1977). "Participation in the design process: A cognitive approach." In D. Stokols (ed.), *Perspectives on environment and behavior: Theory, research and application.* New York: Plenum Press, pp. 221–233.

Kaplan, S., and Kaplan, R. (1982). "The transfer of information." *Cognition and environment: Functioning in an uncertain world.* New York: Praeger, pp. 177–196. (Republished by Ulrich's, Ann Arbor, MI: 1989.)

Kaplan, S., and Kaplan, R. (1989). "The visual environment: Public participation in design and planning." *Journal of Social Issues* 45: 59–86.

Kearney, A. R. (1996). "A tool for small experiments concerning people's understanding of environmental issues." In J. L. Nasar and B. B. Brown (eds.), *Public and private places: Proceedings of the twenty-seventh annual conference of the Environmental Design Research Association.* Edmund, OK: EDRA.

Magill, A. W. (1994). "What people see in managed and natural landscapes." *Journal of Forestry* 92(9): 12–16.

Miller, P. A. (1984). *Visual preference and implications for coastal manage-*

ment: A perceptual study of the British Columbia shoreline. Unpublished doctoral dissertation, University of Michigan, Ann Arbor.

Morrish, W. R., and Brown, C. (1994). *Planning to stay: A collaborative project.* Minneapolis, MN: Milkweed Editions.

National Park Service. (1995). *Heritage trails: Strengthening a regional community.* Denver, CO: Partnerships Branch, United States Department of Interior.

Nohl, W. (1984). "Traces of a participatory aesthetics in urban open spaces." In D. Duerk and D. Cambell (eds.), *The challenge of diversity: Proceedings of the Environmental Design Research Association 15th Annual Conference.* San Luis Obispo: California Polytechnic State University, pp. 269.

Perkins, D. D.; Florin, P.; Rich, R. C.; and Wandersman, A. (1990). "Participation and the social and physical environment of residential blocks: Crime and community context." *Journal of Community Psychology* 18(1): 83–115.

Petit, J., and Gangloff, D. (1995). "The megafauna: People of the urban ecosystem." *Urban Forests* 14: 10–17.

Schroeder, H. W. (1986). "Estimating park tree densities to maximize landscape esthetics." *Journal of Environmental Management* 23: 325– 333.

Schroeder, H. W. (in press). "Volunteers' motivations and values as reflected in ecosystem stewardship newsletters." *Proceedings of the 15th North American Prairie Conference.* St. Charles, Illinois, October 23–26, 1996.

Schroeder, H. W., and Green, T. L. (1985). "Public preference for tree density in a municipal forest program." *Journal of Arboriculture* 11: 272–277.

Sullivan, W. C. (1994). "Perceptions of the rural-urban fringe: Citizen preferences for natural and developed settings." *Landscape and Urban Planning* 29: 85–101.

Sullivan, W. C. (1996). "Cluster housing at the rural-urban fringe: The search for adequate and satisfying places to live." *Journal of Architectural and Planning Research* 13(4): 291–309.

Sullivan, W. C.; Kuo, F. E.; and Prabhu, M. (1996). "Assessing the impact of environmental impact statements on citizens." *Environmental Impact Assessment Review* 16(3): 171–182.

Sullivan, W. C.; Kuo, F. E.; and Prabhu, M. (1997). "Communicating with citizens: The power of photosimulations and simple editing." *Environmental Impact Assessment Review* 17(3): 295–310.

Vachta, K. E., and McDonough, M. H. (1996). "Applications of social forestry in the urban United States: Community outcomes of the urban resources initiative in Detroit." *Proceedings of the Sixth International Symposium on Society and Resource Management.* University Park: Pennsylvania State University, pp. 185–186.

Wandersman, A. (1979). "User participation: A study of types of participation, effects, mediators, and individual differences." *Environment and Behavior* 11(2): 185–208.

Wandersman, A. (1987). "Research on citizen participation." *Participation Network* 5: 22–25.

Weber, W.W. (1980). *Comparison of media for public participation in natural environmental planning*. Unpublished doctoral dissertation, University of Michigan, Ann Arbor.

Westphal, L. M. (1993). "Why trees? Urban forestry volunteers values and motivations." In *Managing urban and high use recreation settings*. St. Paul, MN: USDA Forest Service, General Technical Report NC–163, pp. 19–23.

Westphal, L. M., and Childs, G. (1994). "Overcoming obstacles: Creating volunteer partnerships." *Journal of Forestry* 92(10): 28–32.

Wisner, B.; Stea, D.; and Kruks, S. (1994). "Participatory and action research methods." In E. H. Zube and G. T. Moore (eds.) *Advances in environment, behavior, and design*, vol. 3. New York: Plenum Press.

Chapter 11: Putting It Together

Skelton, R. (1994). "Harlem green-aissance." *Amicus Journal* (Fall): pp. 14–17.

Readings: Alphabetic

Acredolo, L. P. (1982). "The familiarity factor in spatial research." *New Directions for Childhood Development* 15: 19–30.

Acredolo, L. P. (1990). "Behavioral approaches to spatial orientation in infancy." Conference of the National Institute of Mental Health. Catalogued in the *Annals of the New York Academy of Sciences* 608: 596–612.

Adler, J. (1984). "Harvest comes to Brooklyn." *Newsweek,* October 15, p. 17.

Alexander, C.; Ishikawa S.; and Silverstein, M. (1977). *A pattern language.* New York: Oxford University Press.

Allen, G. L., and Kirasic, K. C. (1985). "Effects of the cognitive organization of route knowledge on judgment of macrospatial distance." *Memory and Cognition* 13: 218–227.

Altman, I., and Zube, E. H. (1989). *Public places and spaces.* New York: Plenum Press.

Allton, D. J., and Lieber, S. R. (1983). "Attributes of Chicago trail areas." *Leisure Science* 5(3): 197–220.

Ames, R. G. (1980). "Urban tree planting programs: A sociological perspective." *Hortscience* 15(2): 135–137.

Anderson, E. (1978). *Visual resource assessment:Local perceptions of familiar natural environments.* Unpublished doctoral dissertation, University of Michigan, Ann Arbor.

Anderson, L. M.; Mulligan, B. E.; Goodman, L. S.; and Regen, H. Z. (1983). "Effects of sounds on preferences for outdoor settings." *Environment and Behavior* 15(5): 539–566.

Anderson, L. M., and Schroeder, H. W. (1983). "Application of wildland scenic assessment methods to the urban landscape." *Landscape Planning* 10: 219–237.

Aoki, Y.; Yasuoka, Y.; and Naito, M. (1985). "Assessing the impression of streetside greenery." *Landscape Research* 10: 9–13.

Appleton, J. (1975). *The experience of landscape.* London: John Wiley.

Appleton, J. (1984). "Prospects and refugees re-visited." *Landscape Journal* 3: 91–103.

Appleyard, D. (1978). "Styles and methods of structuring a city." In S. Kaplan and R. Kaplan (eds.), *Humanscape: Environments for people.* Belmont, CA: Duxbury. (Republished by Ulrich's, Ann Arbor, MI: 1982.)

Arthur, P., and Passini, R. (1992). *Wayfinding: People, signs and architecture.* New York: McGraw-Hill.

Axelsson-Lindgren, C., and Sorte, G. (1987). "Public response to differences between visually distinguishable forest stands in a recreation area." *Landscape and Urban Planning* 14: 211–217.

Balling, J. D., and Falk, J. H. (1982). "Development of visual preference for natural environments." *Environment and Behavior* 14: 5–28.

Bardwell, L. V. (1991a). "Problem-framing: A perspective on environmental problem-solving." *Environmental Management* 15(5): 603–612.

Bardwell, L. V. (1991b). "Success stories: Imagery by example." *Journal of Environmental Education* 23(1): 5–10.

Bardwell, L. V. (1996). "The human face of environmental problem solving: Insights for environmental success stories." In J. L. Nasar and B. B. Brown (eds.), *Public and private places: Proceedings of the twenty-seventh annual conference of the Environmental Design Research Association.* Edmund, OK: EDRA, pp. 144–150.

Bassett, T. J. (1979). "Reaping on the margins: A century of community gardening in America." *Landscape* 25: 1–8.

Bixler, R.D.; Carlisle, C. L.; and Floyd, M. F. (1995). "Wayfinding aids: Getting the novice into the woods." *Legacy* 12: 25–29.

Bixler, R. D.; Carlisle, C. L.; Hammitt, W. E.; and Floyd, M. F. (1994). "Observed fears and discomforts among urban students on school field trips to wildland areas." *Journal of Environmental Education* 26: 24–33.

Bixler, R. D., and Floyd, M. F. (1997). "Nature is scary, disgusting and uncomfortable." *Environment and Behavior* 29(4): 443–467.

Bixler, R. D.; Floyd, M. F.; and Hammitt, W. E. (1995). "Feared stimuli are expected in specific situations: Using an expectancy approach and situationalism in self-report measures of fear." *Journal of Clinical Psychology* 51(4): 544–547.

Blades, M. (1991). "Wayfinding theory and research: The need for a new approach." In D. M. Mark and A. U. Frank (eds.), *Cognitive and linguistic aspects of geographic science.* Dordrecht, Netherlands: Kluwer Academic Publishers, pp. 137–165.

Bluestein, N., and Acredolo, L. (1979). "Developmental changes in map-reading skills." *Child Development* 50: 691–697.

Bradley, G. A. (1996a). "Small experiments for the protection of the scenic resource." In J. L. Nasar, and B. B. Brown (eds.), *Public and private places: Proceedings of the twenty-seventh annual conference of the Environmental Design Research Association.* Edmund, OK: EDRA.

Bradley, G. A. (1996b). *Forest aesthetics: Harvest practices in visually sensitive areas.* Olympia, WA: Washington Forest Protection Association.

Brower, S. (1977). *The design of neighborhood parks.* Baltimore: City Planning Commission.

Brower, S.; Dockett, K.; and Taylor, R. (1983). "Residents' perceptions of territorial features and perceived local threat." *Environment and Behavior* 15: 419–426.

Brower, S. N. (1988). *Design in familiar places: What makes home environments look good.* New York: Praeger.

Brunson, L.; Kuo, F. E.; and Sullivan, W. C. (under review). "Sowing the seeds of community: Greening and gardening in inner-city neighborhoods." *American Journal of Community Psychology.*

Canin, L. H. (1992). *Psychological restoration among AIDS caregivers: Maintaining self-care.* Unpublished doctoral dissertation, University of Michigan, Ann Arbor.

Cantor, J., and Omdahl, B. L. (1991). "Effects of fictional media depictions of realistic threats on children's emotional responses, expectations, worries, and liking for related activities." *Communications Monograph* 58(4): 384–401.

Carr, S.; Francis, M.; Rivlin, L. G.; and Stone, A. M. (1992). *Public space.* Cambridge: Cambridge University Press.

Carr, S., and Lynch, K. (1981). "Open space: Freedom and control." In L. Taylor (ed.), *Urban open spaces.* New York: Rizzoli.

Chavis, D. M.; Stucky, P. E.; and Wandersman, A. (1983). "Returning basic research to the community: A relationship between scientist and citizen." *American Psychologist* 38(4): 424–434.

Chenney, T.; Hofmockel, M.; and Ryan, R. (1985). *Japanese gardens: Traditions in design.* Unpublished Senior Project Report, Landscape Architecture Department, California Polytechnic State University, San Luis Obispo, CA.

Chenoweth, R. E., and Gobster, P. H. (1990). "The nature and ecology of aesthetic experiences in the landscape." *Landscape Journal* 9: 1–8.

Cimprich, B. E. (1990). *Attentional fatigue and restoration in individuals with cancer.* Unpublished doctoral dissertation, University of Michigan, Ann Arbor.

Cimprich, B. E. (1992). "Attentional fatigue following breast cancer surgery." *Nursing and Health* 15(3): 199–207.

Clarkson, J. D. (1970). "Ecology and spatial analysis." *Annals of the Association of American Geographers* 60: 700.

Coeterier, J. F. (1983). "A photo validity test." *Journal of Environmental Psychology* 3: 315–323.

Cohen, S. (1978). "Environmental load and the allocation of attention." In A. Baum, J. Singer, and S. Valins (eds.), *Advances in Environmental Psychology,* vol. 1. Hillsdale: Erlbaum, pp. 1–29.

Coley, R. L.; Kuo, F. E.; and Sullivan, W. C. (1997). "Where does community grow? The social context created by nature in urban public housing." *Environment and Behavior* 29(4): 468–494.

Cooper-Marcus, C., and Sarkissian, W. (1986). *Housing as if people mattered: Site design guidelines for medium-density housing.* Berkeley: University of California Press.

Cornell, E. H.; Heth, C. D.; and Broda, L. S. (1989). "Children's wayfinding: Response to instructions to use environmental landmarks." *Developmental Psychology* 25(5): 755–764.

Cullen, G. (1971). *The concise townscape.* New York, Van Nostrand Reinhold.

Cundiff, B. (1996). "Invasion of primacy." *Nature Canada* 25(2): 32–37.

Darragh, A. J.; Peterson, G. L.; and Dwyer, J. F. (1983). "Travel cost models at the urban scale." *Journal of Leisure Research* 15(2): 89–94.

Deardorff, H. (1996). "Redesigning the small town mainstreet: Participation, small experiments and unique solutions." In J. L. Nasar and B. B. Brown (eds.), *Public and private places: Proceedings of the twenty-seventh annual conference of the Environmental Design Research Association*. Edmund, OK: EDRA.

Devlin, A. S., and Bernstein, J. (1995). "Interactive wayfinding: Uses of cues by men and women." *Journal of Environmental Psychology* 15(1): 23–28.

Devlin, A. S.; Morton, J.; Zaff, J.; Freedland, C.; and Mendez, N. (1996). "Dormitory environments, daily stress, and environmental preference." In J. L. Nasar and B. B. Brown (eds.), *Public and private places: Proceedings of the twenty-seventh annual conference of the Environmental Design Research Association*. Edmund, OK: EDRA, pp. 98–105.

De Young, R., and Monroe, M. C. (1996). "Some fundamentals of engaging stories." *Environmental Education Research* 2: 171–179.

Dravnieks, G., and Pitcher, P. C. (1982). *Public participation in resource planning: Selected literature abstracts*. Berkeley, CA: United States Department of Agriculture, Forest Service.

Dreyfus, H. L., and Dreyfus, S. E. (1984). "Mindless machines: Computers don't think like experts, and never will." *The Sciences* 24: 18–22.

Dwyer, J. F., and Hutchison, R. (1990). "Outdoor recreation participation and preferences by black and white Chicago households." In J. Vining (ed.), *Social science and natural resources management*. Boulder, CO: Westview Press.

Dwyer, J. F.; Hutchison, R.; and Wendling, R. C. (1981). "Participation of outdoor recreation by black and white Chicago households." Presented at the National Recreation and Park Association Symposium on Leisure Research, Minneapolis, October 26, 1981.

Dwyer, J. F.; McPherson E. G.; Schroeder, H. W.; and Rowntree, R. A. (1992). "Assessing the benefits and costs of the urban forest." *Journal of Arboriculture* 18(5): 227–234.

Dwyer, J. F., and Schroeder, H. W. (1994). "The human dimensions of urban forestry." *Journal of Forestry* 92(10): 12–15.

Dwyer, J. F.; Schroeder, H. W.; and Gobster, P. H. (1991). "The significance of urban trees and forests: Toward a deeper understanding of values." *Journal of Arboriculture* 17(10): 276–284.

Dwyer, J. F.; Schroeder, H. W.; and Gobster, P. H. (1994). "The deep significance of urban trees and forests." In R. H. Platt, R. A. Rowntree, and P. C. Muick (eds.), *Preserving and restoring biodiversity*. Amherst: University of Massachusetts Press, pp. 137–150.

Ellsworth, J. C. (1982). *Visual assessment of rivers and marshes: An examination of the relationship of visual units, perceptual variables, and preference*. Unpublished master's thesis, Utah State University, Logan.

Falk, J. H., and Dierking, L. D. (1992). *The museum experience*. Washington, DC: Whalesback Books.

Field, D. R., and Wagar, J. A. (1976). "People and interpretation." In G. Sharpe (ed.), *Interpreting the environment.* New York: John Wiley, pp. 43–56.

Fischhoff, B.; Lichtenstein, S.; Slovic, P.; Derby, S. L.; and Keeney, R. L. (1981). *Acceptable risk.* New York: Cambridge University Press. (See chapter 4: Professional judgment.)

Fisher, B. S., and Nasar, J. L. (1992). "Fear of crime in relation to three exterior site features: Prospect, refuge, and escape." *Environment and Behavior* 24: 35–65.

Flagler, J., and Poincelot, R. P. (1994). *People-plant relationships: Setting research priorities.* New York: Food Products Press.

Flink, C., and Searns, R. M. (1993). *Greenways: A guide to planning, design, and development.* Washington, DC: Island Press.

Florin, P., and Wandersman, A. (1990). "An introduction to citizen participation, voluntary organizations, and community development: Insights for empowerment through research." *American Journal of Community Psychology* 18(1): 41–54.

Forrest, D., and Castner, H. W. (1985). "Design and perception of point symbols for tourist maps." *Cartographic Journal* 22: 11–19.

Fox, T.; Koeppel, I.; and Kellam, S. (1985). *Struggle for space: The greening of New York City, 1970–1984.* New York: Neighborhood Open Space Coalition.

Francis, M. (1987a). "Meanings attached to a city park and a community garden in Sacramento." *Landscape Research* 12(1): 8–12.

Francis, M. (1987b). "Urban open spaces." In E. H. Zube and G. T. Moore (eds.), *Advances in environment, behavior, and design,* vol. 1. New York: Plenum Press.

Francis, M. (1987c). "The making of democratic streets." In A. Vernez-Moudon (ed.), *Streets are public.* New York: Van Nostrand Reinhold.

Francis, M. (1988). "Negotiating between children and adult design values in open space projects." *Design Studies* 9(2): 187–195.

Francis, M. (1989). "Control as a dimension of public-space quality." In I. Altman and E. H. Zube (eds.), *Public places and spaces.* New York: Plenum Press, pp. 147–169.

Francis, M. (1995). *The healing dimensions of people–plant relations: A research symposium.* Davis: University of California Center for Design Research.

Francis, M.; Cashdan, L.; and Paxson, L. (1984). *Community open spaces.* Washington, DC: Island Press.

Francis, M., and Hester, R. T., Jr. (1990). *The meaning of gardens.* Cambridge, MA: MIT Press.

Franck, K. A., and Paxson, L. (1989). "Women and urban public space: Research, design, and policy issues." In I. Altman and E. H. Zube (eds.), *Public places and spaces.* New York: Plenum Press, pp. 121–146.

Frewald, D. B. (1989). *Preferences for older buildings: A psychological approach to architectural design.* Unpublished doctoral dissertation, University of Michigan, Ann Arbor.

Fried, M. (1963). "Grieving for a lost home." In L. J. Duhl (ed.) *The urban condition: People and policy in the metropolis.* New York: Basic Books.

Fritschen, J. M., and Stynes, D. J. (1980). "Interpretation for urban audiences." In *Proceedings of the Association of Interpretative Naturalists Workshop.* Cape Cod, MA.

Furbrey, R., and Goodchild, B. (1986). "Attitudes to environment." *Housing* 22(3): 20–21.

Gärling, T., and Golledge, R. G. (1989). "Environmental perception and cognition." In E. H. Zube and G. T. Moore (eds.), *Advances in environment, behavior, and design.* New York: Plenum Press.

Gärling, T.; Lindberg, E.; Carreriras, M.; and Böök, A. (1986). "Reference systems in cognitive maps." *Journal of Environmental Psychology* 6: 1–18.

Getz, D. A., and Kielbaso, J. J. (1982). "Inner city preference for trees and urban forestry programs." *Journal of Arboriculture* 8: 258–263.

Gimblett, R. H.; Itami, R. M.; and Fitzgibbon, J. E. (1985). "Mystery in an information processing model of landscape preference." *Landscape Journal* 4: 87–95.

Gluck, M. (1991). "Making sense of human wayfinding: Review of cognitive and linguistic knowledge for personal navigation with a new research direction." In D. M. Mark and A. U. Frank (eds.), *Cognitive and linguistic aspects of geographic space.* Dordrecht, Netherlands: Kluwer Academic Publishers, pp. 117–135.

Gobster, P. H. (1991a). "Forest vegetation in urban parks: Perceptions of inner city children." In G. A. Vander Stoep (ed.), *Proceedings of the 1991 Northeastern Recreation Research Symposium.* Chicago, IL: USDA Forest Service, General Technical Report NE–160, pp. 209–214.

Gobster, P. H. (1991b). "Urban park trail use: An observational approach." In G. A. Vander Stoep (ed.), *Proceedings of the 1991 Northeastern Recreation Research Symposium.* Chicago, IL: USDA Forest Service, General Technical Report NE–160, pp. 215–221.

Gobster, P. H. (1995). "Perceptions and use of a metropolitan greenway system for recreation." *Landscape and Urban Planning* 33: 401–413.

Gobster, P. H. (1997). "The Chicago wildreness and its critics. Part III, the other side: A survey of arguments." *Restoration and Management Notes* 15(1): 32–37.

Godbey, G., and Blaze, M. (1983). "Old people in urban parks." *Journal of Leisure Research* 15: 229–244.

Gold, S. M. (1972). "Nonuse of neighborhood parks." *Journal of the American Institute of Planners* 38: 369–378.

Golledge, R. G. (1991). "Environmental cognition." In D. Stokols and I. Altman (eds.), *Handbook of environmental psychology,* vol. 1. Malabar, FL: Krieger, pp. 131–174.

Golledge, R. G. (1993). "Geographical perspectives on spatial cognition." In T. Gärling and R. G. Golledge (eds.), *Behavior and environment: Psychological and geographical approaches.* Amsterdam: Elsevier Science Publishers, pp. 16–46.

Green Cities Initiative. (1994). *Healing America's cities: How urban parks can make cities safe and healthy.* San Francisco: Trust for Public Land.

Grove, Morgan. (1993). "The urban resources initiative: Community benefits from forestry." In P. H. Gobster (ed.), *Managing urban and high-use recreation settings.* St. Paul, MN: USDA Forest Service, General Technical Report NC–163, pp. 46–49.

Gundry, K. G., and Heberlein, T. A. (1984). *Do public meetings represent the public?* Madison: University of Wisconsin, Rural Sociology Department.

Hammitt, W. E. (1978a). *Visual and user preference for a bog environment.* Unpublished doctoral dissertation, University of Michigan, Ann Arbor.

Hammit, W. E. (1978b). "A visual preference approach to measuring interpretive effectiveness." *Journal of Interpretation* 3(2): 33–37.

Hammitt, W. E. (1979). "Measuring familiarity for natural environments through visual images." In *Proceedings of Our National Landscape Conference.* Berkeley, CA: USDA Forest Service, General Technical Report PSW–35, pp. 217–226.

Hammitt, W. E. (1980). "Designing mystery into landscape-trail experiences." *Journal of Interpretation* 5(1): 16–19.

Hammitt, W. E. (1981). "The familiarity-preference component of on-site recreational experiences." *Leisure Sciences* 4: 177–193.

Hammitt, W. E. (1988). "Visual and management preferences of sightseers." In F. P. Noe and W. E. Hammitt (eds.), *Visual preferences along the Blue Ridge Parkway.* Washington, DC: U.S. Department of Interior, National Park Service, pp. 11–36.

Hammitt, W. E., and Cherem, G. J. (1980). "Photographic perceptions as an on-site tool for designing forest trails." *Southern Journal of Applied Forestry* 4(2): 94–97.

Hammitt, W. E.; Patterson, M. E.; and Noe, F. P. (1994). "Identifying and predicting visual preference of Southern Appalachian Forest recreation vistas." *Journal of Landscape and Urban Planning* 29: 171–183.

Harrison, C.; Limb, M.; and Burgess, J. (1987). "Nature in the city: Popular values for a living world." *Journal of Environmental Management* 25: 347–362.

Hart, R. (1979). *Children's experience of place.* New York: Irvington Publishers.

Hartig, T. (1993). "Testing restorative environments theory." *Dissertation Abstracts International* 54, 08B. (University Microfilms No. 94–02, 422.)

Hartig, T.; Böök, A.; Garvill, J.; Olsson, T.; and Gärling, T. (1996). "Environmental influences on psychological restoration." *Scandinavian Journal of Psychology* 37: 378–393.

Hartig, T., and Evans, G. W. (1993). "Psychological foundations of nature experience." In T. Gärling and R. G. Golledge (eds.), *Behavior and environment: Psychological and geographical approaches.* Amsterdam: Elsevier Science Publishers.

Hartig, T.; Mang, M.; and Evans, G. W. (1991). "The restorative effects of natural environment experience." *Environment and Behavior* 23(1): 3–26.

Hayward, J. (1989). "Urban parks: Research, planning, and social change." In I. Altman and E. H. Zube (eds.), *Public places and spaces*. New York: Plenum Press, pp. 193–216.

Heerwagen, J. H., and Orians, G. H. (1986). "Adaptations to windowlessness: A study of the use of visual decor in windowed and windowless offices." *Environment and Behavior* 18: 623–639.

Hendee, J. C., and Schoenfield. C. (1973). *Human dimensions in wildlife programs*. Rockville, MD: Mercury Press.

Herzog, T. R. (1984). "A cognitive analysis for field-and-forest environments." *Landscape Research* 9: 10–16.

Herzog, T. R. (1985). "A cognitive analysis of preference for waterscapes." *Journal of Environmental Psychology* 5: 225–241.

Herzog, T. R. (1987). "A cognitive analysis of preference for natural environments: Mountains, canyons, and deserts." *Landscape Journal* 6: 140–152.

Herzog, T. R. (1989). "A cognitive analysis of preference for urban nature." *Journal of Environmental Psychology* 9: 27–43.

Herzog, T. R. (1992). "A cognitive analysis of preference for urban spaces." *Journal of Environmental Psychology* 12: 237–248.

Herzog, T. R.; Black, A. M.; Fountaine, K. A.; and Knotts, D. J. (1997). "Reflection and attentional recovery as distinctive benefits of restorative environments." *Journal of Environmental Psychology* 17: 165–170.

Herzog, T.R., and Bosley, P. J. (1992). "Tranquillity and preference as affective qualities of natural environments." *Journal of Environmental Psychology* 12: 115–127.

Herzog, T. R., and Chernick, K. K. (in review). "Tranquillity and danger in urban and natural settings."

Herzog, T. R., and Gale, T. A. (1996). "Preference for urban buildings as a function of age and nature context." *Environment and Behavior* 28:44–72.

Herzog, T. R.; Kaplan, S.; and Kaplan, R. (1976). "The prediction of preference of familiar urban places." *Environment and Behavior* 8: 627–645.

Herzog, T. R.; Kaplan, S.; and Kaplan, R. (1982). "The prediction of preference for unfamiliar urban places." *Population and Environment* 5(1): 43–59.

Herzog, T. R., and Smith, G. A. (1988). "Danger, mystery, and environmental preference." *Environment and Behavior* 20: 320–344.

Hester, R. T., Jr. (1984). *Planning neighborhood space with people*. New York: Van Nostrand Reinhold.

Hester, R. T., Jr. (1990). *Community design primer*. Mendocino, CA: Ridge Times Press.

Hester, R. T., Jr. (1995). "Life, liberty and the pursuit of sustainable happiness." *Places* 9(3): 2–17.

Hester, R. T., Jr. (1996). "Wanted: Local participation with a view." In J. L. Nasar and B. B. Brown (eds.), *Public and private places: Proceedings of the twenty-seventh annual conference of the Environmental Design Research Association*. Edmund, OK: EDRA, pp. 42–52.

Hester, R. T., Jr.; Blazej, N. J.; and Moore, I. S. (1996). "Whose wild? Resolving cultural and biological diversity conflicts in urban wilderness." Paper presented at Council of Educators in Landscape Architecture Annual Conference, Spokane, Washington, August 7–10, 1996.

Hitchmough, J. (1993). "The urban bush." *Landscape Design* 222: 13–17.

Hill, K. A. (1992). "Spatial competence of elderly hunters." *Environment and Behavior* 24: 779–794.

Homel, R., and Burns, A. (1987). "Is this a good place to grow up in? Neighbourhood quality and children's evaluations." *Landscape and Urban Planning* 14: 101–116.

Hubbard, H. V., and Kimball, T. (1959). *An introduction to the study of landscape design.* New England: Cuneo Press, pp. 82–83.

Hudspeth, T. R. (1986). "Visual preference as a tool for facilitating citizen participation in urban waterfront revitalization." *Journal of Environmental Management* 23: 373–385.

Im, S. B. (1984). "Visual preferences in enclosed urban spaces." *Environment and Behavior* 16: 235–262.

Ito, T. (1973). *Space and illusion in a Japanese garden* New York: Weatherhill Press.

Ives, S. (1977). "A conversation with Martin J. Rosen." *Land and People* 9: 1, 30.

Kaplan, R. (1973a). "Some psychological benefits of gardening." *Environment and Behavior* 5: 145–161.

Kaplan, R. (1973b). "Predictors of environmental preference: Designers and 'clients'." In W. F. E. Peiser (ed.), *Environmental design research.* Stroudsburg, PA: Dowden, Hutchinson, and Ross.

Kaplan, R. (1976). "Way-finding in the natural environment." In G. T. Moore and R. G. Golledge (eds.), *Environmental knowing: Theories, perspectives, and methods.* Stroudsburg, PA: Dowden, Hutchinson, and Ross.

Kaplan, R. (1977). "Preference and everyday nature: Method and application." In D. Stokols (ed.), *Perspectives on environment and behavior: Theory, research, and applications.* New York: Plenum Press.

Kaplan, R. (1978). "Participation in environmental design: Some considerations and a case study." In S. Kaplan and R. Kaplan (eds.), *Humanscape: Environments for people.* Belmont, CA: Duxbury. (Republished by Ulrich's, Ann Arbor, MI: 1982.)

Kaplan, R. (1980). "Citizen participation in the design and evaluation of a park." *Environment and Behavior* 12: 494–507.

Kaplan, R. (1983). "The role of nature in the urban context." In I. Altman and J. F. Wohlwill (eds.), *Behavior and the Natural Environment.* New York: Plenum Press.

Kaplan, R. (1984a). "Dominant and variant values in environmental preference." In A. S. Devlin and S. L. Taylor (eds.), *Environmental preference and landscape preference.* New London: Connecticut College Press.

Kaplan, R. (1984b). "Assessing human concerns for environmental decision-making." In S. L. Hart, G.A. Enk, and W. F. Hornick (eds.), *Improving impact assessment: Increasing the relevance and utilization of technical and scientific information.* Boulder, CO: Westview Press, pp. 37–56.

Kaplan, R. (1984c). "Impact of urban nature: A theoretical analysis." *Urban Ecology* 8: 189–197.

Kaplan, R. (1985a). "Nature at the doorstep: Residential satisfaction and the nearby environment." *Journal of Architectural and Planning Research* 2: 115–127.

Kaplan, R. (1985b). "The analysis of perception via preference: A strategy for studying how the environment is experienced." *Landscape Planning* 12: 161–176.

Kaplan, R. (1987). "Simulation models and participation: Designers and 'clients'." In J. Harvey and D. Henning (eds.), *Public environments.* Washington, DC: Proceedings of the Environmental Design Research Association, pp. 96–102.

Kaplan, R. (1990). "Collaboration from a cognitive perspective: Sharing models across expertise." In R. I. Selby, K. H. Anthony, J. Choi, and B. Orland (eds.), *Coming of age.* Oklahoma City: Environmental Design Research Association, pp. 45–51.

Kaplan, R. (1992). "The psychological benefits of nearby nature." In D. Relf (ed.), *The role of horticulture in human well-being and social development.* Portland, OR: Timber Press.

Kaplan, R. (1993a). "Physical models in decision making for design: Theoretical and methodological issues." In R. W. Marans and D. Stokols (eds.), *Environmental simulation: Research and policy issues.* New York: Plenum Press.

Kaplan, R. (1993b). "The role of nature in the context of the workplace." *Landscape and Urban Planning* 26: 193–201.

Kaplan, R. (1993c). "Environmental appraisal, human needs, and a sustainable future." In T. Gärling and R. G. Golledge (eds.), *Behavior and environment: Psychological and geographical approaches.* Amsterdam: Elsevier Science Publishers, pp. 117–140.

Kaplan, R. (1995). "Informational issues: A perspective on human needs and inclinations." In G. A. Bradley (ed.), *Urban forest landscapes: Integrating multidisciplinary perspectives.* Seattle: University of Washington Press, pp. 60–71.

Kaplan, R. (1996). "The small experiment: Achieving more with less." In J. L. Nasar and B. B. Brown (eds.), *Public and private places: Proceedings of the twenty-seventh annual conference of the Environmental Design Research Association.* Edmund, OK: EDRA, pp. 170–174.

Kaplan, R.; Bardwell, L. V.; Ford, H. A.; and Kaplan, S. (1996). "The corporate back-40: Employee benefits of wildlife enhancement efforts on corporate land." *Human Dimensions of Wildlife* 1(2): 1–13.

Kaplan, R., and Herbert, E. J. (1987). "Cultural and sub-cultural comparisons in preference for natural settings." *Landscape and Urban Planning* 14: 291–293.

Kaplan, R., and Herbert, E. J. (1988). "Familiarity and preference: A cross-cultural analysis." In J. L. Nasar (ed.), *Environmental aesthetics: Theory, research and application.* New York: Cambridge University Press, pp. 379–389.

Kaplan, R., and Kaplan, S. (1989). *The experience of nature: A psychological perspective.* New York: Cambridge University Press. (Republished by Ulrich's, Ann Arbor, MI: 1996.)

Kaplan, R.; Kaplan, S.; and Brown, T. J. (1989). "Environmental preference: A comparison of four domains of predictors." *Environment and Behavior* 21: 509–530.

Kaplan, R., and Talbot, J. F. (1988). "Ethnicity and preference for natural settings: A review and recent findings." *Landscape and Urban Planning* 15: 107–117.

Kaplan, S. (1973). "Cognitive maps in perception and thought." In R. M. Downs and D. Stea (eds.), *Image and environment.* Chicago, IL: Aldine, pp. 63–78.

Kaplan, S. (1975). "An informal model for the prediction of preference." In E. H. Zube, R. O. Brush, and J. G. Fabos (eds.), *Landscape assessment: Values, perceptions and resources.* Stroudsburg, PA: Dowden, Hutchinson, and Ross, pp. 92–101.

Kaplan, S. (1977). "Participation in the design process: A cognitive approach." In D. Stokols (ed.), *Perspectives on environment and behavior: Theory, research and application.* New York: Plenum Press, pp. 221–233.

Kaplan, S. (1978). "Attention and fascination: The search for cognitive clarity." In S. Kaplan and R. Kaplan (eds.), *Humanscape: Environments for people.* Belmont, CA: Duxbury. (Republished by Ulrich's, Ann Arbor, MI: 1982.)

Kaplan, S. (1983). "A model of person-environment compatibility." *Environment and Behavior* 15(3): 311–332.

Kaplan, S. (1985). "Cognition and affect in environmental learning." *Children's Environmental Quarterly* 2(3): 19–21.

Kaplan, S. (1987). "Mental fatigue and the designed environment." In J. Harvey and D. Henning (eds.), *Public environments.* Washington, DC: Environmental Design Research Association, pp. 55–60.

Kaplan, S. (1988). "Perception and landscape: Conceptions and misconceptions." In J. L. Nasar (ed.), *Environmental aesthetics: Theory, research, and application.* New York: Cambridge University Press, pp. 45–55.

Kaplan, S. (1989). "Past environments and past stories in human effectiveness and well being." In G. Hardie, R. Moore, and H. Sanoff (eds.), *Changing paradigms.* Oklahoma City: Environmental Design Research Association, pp. 223–228.

Kaplan, S. (1991). "Beyond rationality: Clarity-based decision making." In T. Gärling and G. Evans (eds.), *Environment, cognition and action: An integrative multidisciplinary approach.* New York: Oxford University Press, pp. 171–190.

Kaplan, S. (1992a). "Environmental preference in a knowledge-seeking knowledge-using organism." In J. H. Barkow, L. Cosmides, and J. Tooby (eds.), *The adapted mind.* New York: Oxford University Press, pp. 535–552.

Kaplan, S. (1992b). "The restorative environment: Nature and human experience." In D. Relf (ed.), *The role of horticulture in human well-being and social development.* Portland, OR: Timber Press, pp. 134–142.

Kaplan, S. (1993). "The role of natural environment aesthetics in the restorative experience." In P. H. Gobster (ed.), *Managing urban and high-use recreation settings*. St. Paul, MN: USDA Forest Service, General Technical Report NC–163, pp. 46–49.

Kaplan, S. (1995a). "The urban forest as a source of psychological well-being." In G. A. Bradley (ed.), *Urban forest landscapes: Integrating multidisciplinary perspectives*. Seattle: University of Washington Press.

Kaplan, S. (1995b). "The restorative benefits of nature: Toward an integrative framework." *Journal of Environmental Psychology* 15: 169–182.

Kaplan, S., and Kaplan, R., eds. (1978). *Humanscape: Environments for people*. Belmont, CA: Duxbury. (Republished by Ulrich's, Ann Arbor, MI: 1982.)

Kaplan, S., and Kaplan, R. (1982). *Cognition and environment: Functioning in an uncertain world*. New York: Praeger. (Republished by Ulrich's, Ann Arbor, MI: 1989.)

Kaplan, S., and Kaplan, R. (1989). "The visual environment: Public participation in design and planning." *Journal of Social Issues* 45: 59–86.

Kaplan, S.; Kaplan, R.; and Wendt, J. S. (1972). "Rated preference and complexity for natural and urban visual material." *Perception and Psychophysics* 12: 354–356.

Kaplan, S., and Peterson, C. (1993). "Health and environment: A psychological analysis." *Landscape and Urban Planning* 26: 17–23.

Kaplan, S., and Talbot, J. F. (1983). "Psychological benefits of a wilderness experience." In I. Altman and J. F. Wohlwill (eds.), *Behavior and the natural environment*. New York: Plenum, pp. 163–203.

Keane, T. D. (1990). *The role of familiarity in landscape aesthetics: A study of tallgrass prairie landscapes*. Unpublished doctoral dissertation, University of Michigan, Ann Arbor.

Kearney, A. R. (1994). "Understanding global change: A cognitive perspective on communication through stories." *Climatic Change* 27: 419–441.

Kearney, A. R. (1996a). "A tool for small experiments concerning people's understanding of environmental issues." In J. L. Nasar and B. B. Brown (eds.), *Public and private places: Proceedings of the twenty-seventh annual conference of the Environmental Design Research Association*. Edmund, OK: EDRA.

Kearney, A. R. (1996b). "Public attitudes and preferences regarding the Indian River." Research report submitted to USDA Forest Service, North Central Forest Experiment Station, East Lansing, MI.

Kearney, A. R. (1997). "Expertise and cognitive clarity." *Some implications of cognitive map theory for environmental problem solving and decision making*. Unpublished doctoral dissertation, University of Michigan, Ann Arbor.

Kearney, A. R., and Kaplan, S. (1997). "Toward a methodology for the measurement of the knowledge structures of ordinary people: The conceptual content cognitive map (3CM)." *Environment and Behavior* 29: 579–617.

Kent, R. L., and Elliot, C. L. (1995). "Scenic routes linking and protecting natural and cultural landscape features: A greenway skeleton." *Landscape and Urban Planning* 33: 341–356.

Keyes, B. E., and Hammitt W. E. (1984). "Visitor reaction to interpretive signs on a destination-oriented forest trail." *Journal of Interpretation* 9(1): 11–17.

Kirasic, K. C., and Mathes, E. A. (1990). "Effects of different means for conveying environmental information on elderly adults' spatial cognition and behavior." *Environment and Behavior* 22: 591–607.

Kirkby, M. (1989). "Nature as a refuge in children's environments." *Children's Environments Quarterly* 6(1): 7–12.

Korpela, K., and Hartig, T. (1996). "Restorative qualities of favorite places." *Journal of Environmental Psychology* 16: 221–233.

Kroh, D., and Gimblett, R. H. (1992). "Comparing live experience with pictures in articulating landscape preference." *Landscape Research* 17(2): 58–69.

Kuo, F. E. (1995). *Facilitating learning and adaptation in unfamiliar environments: Maps, spatial orientation, and the university.* Unpublished doctoral dissertation, University of Michigan, Ann Arbor.

Kuo, F. E.; Bacaicoa, M.; and Sullivan, W. C. (1998). "Transforming inner-city landscapes: Trees, sense of safety, and preference in urban public housing." *Environment and Behavior* 30(1): 28–59.

Kuo, F. E.; Sullivan, W. C.; Coley, R. L.; and Brunson, L. (under review). "Fertile ground for community: Inner-city neighborhood common spaces." *American Journal of Community Psychology.*

Lazarus, J., and Symonds, M. (1993). "Contrasting effects of protective and obstructive cover on avian vigilance." *Animal Behavior* 43: 519–521.

Levin, J. (1977). *Riverside preference: On-site and photographic reactions.* Unpublished master's thesis, University of Michigan, Ann Arbor.

Levine, M. (1982). "You are here maps: Psychological considerations." *Environment and Behavior* 14(2): 221–237.

Levine, M.; Marchan, I.; and Hanley, G. (1984). "Placement and misplacement of you-are-here maps." *Environment and Behavior* 16(2): 139–157.

Lewis, C. A. (1978). "Nature city." In S. Kaplan and R. Kaplan (eds.), *Humanscape: Environments for people.* Belmont, CA: Duxbury, pp. 448–453. (Republished by Ulrich's, Ann Arbor, MI: 1982.)

Lewis, C. A. (1996). *Green nature / human nature: The meaning of plants in our lives.* Urbana: University of Illinois Press.

Lieber, S. R., and Allton, D. J. (1983). "Modeling trail area evaluations in metropolitan Chicago." *Journal of Leisure Research* 15(3): 184–202.

Lieber, S.R., and Fesenmaier, D. R. (1985). "Physical and social conditions affecting recreational site preferences." *Environment and Planning A* 17: 1613–1625.

Little, C. E. (1990). *Greenways for America.* Baltimore, MD: Johns Hopkins University Press.

Loomis, R. (1987). *Visitor evaluation.* Nashville, TN: American Association for State and Local History.

Louviere, J. J.; Anderson, D. A.; and Louviere, C. H. (1991). *Bike trail choice among Chicago area trail users.* North Central Forest Experiment Stations, Chicago, IL: USDA Forest Service, unpublished final report.

Lynch, K. (1960). *The image of the city.* Cambridge, MA: MIT Press.

Lynch, K. (1977). *Growing up in cities: Studies of the spatial environments of adolescence in Cracow, Melbourne, Mexico City, Salta, Toluca, and Warszawa.* Cambridge, MA: MIT Press.

Lynch, K. (1984). *Site planning,* 3rd edition. Cambridge, MA: MIT Press.

Mackay-Yarnal, C. M., and Coulson, M. R. C. (1982). "Recreational map design and map use: An experiment." *Cartographic Journal* 19(1): 16–27.

Magill, A. W. (1994). "What people see in managed and natural landscapes." *Journal of Forestry* 92(9): 12–16.

Malakoff, D. (1995). "What good is community greening?" *Community Greening Review* 5: 4–11.

Mander, J. (1978). *Four arguments for the elimination of television.* New York: Morrow Quill.

Mandler, G. (1975a). "Consciousness: Respectful, useful, and probably necessary." In R. L. Solso (ed.), *Information processing and cognitive psychology.* Hillsdale, NJ: Erlbaum.

Mandler, G. (1975b). "Memory storage and retrieval: Some limits on the research of attention and consciousness." In P. M. Rabbitt and S. Dornic (eds.), *Attention and performance,* vol. 5. London: Academic Press.

Martin, R. D. (1993). *Suburban residents' perception of wildlife habitat patches and corridors in their neighborhoods.* Unpublished thesis, University of Minnesota.

McAndrew, F. T. (1993). *Environmental psychology.* Pacific Grove, CA: Brooks/Cole Publishing.

McIntyre, N.; Cuskelly, G.; and Auld, C. (1991). "The benefits of urban parks." *Australian Parks and Recreation* 27: 11–18.

Mertes, J. D., and Hall, J. R. (1995). *Park, recreation, open space and greenway guidelines.* Arlington, VA: National Recreation and Park Association.

Metro, L. J.; Dwyer, J. F.; and Dreschler, E. S. (1981). *Forest experiences of fifth-grade Chicago public school students.* St. Paul, MN: USDA Forest Service, Research Paper NC–21.

Michael, S. E., and Hull IV, R. B. (1994). *The effects of vegetation on crime in urban parks.* Blacksburg, VA: Department of Forestry and Wildlife Resources, Virginia Polytechnic and State University.

Milgram, S. (1970). "The experience of living in cities." *Science* 167: 1461–1468.

Miller, P. A. (1984). *Visual preference and implications for coastal management: A perceptual study of the British Columbia shoreline.* Unpublished doctoral dissertation, University of Michigan, Ann Arbor.

Monmonier, M. S. (1996). *How to lie with maps.* Chicago: University of Illinois Press.

Montello, D. R. (1991). "Spatial orientation and angularity of urban routes: A field study." *Environment and Behavior* 23: 47–69.

Moore, E. O. (1981). "A prison environment's effect on health care service demands." *Journal of Environmental Systems* 11: 17–34.

Moore, R. C. (1986). *Childhood domain: Play and place in child development.* London: Croom Helm.

Morrish, W. R., and Brown, C. (1994). *Planning to stay: A collaborative project.* Minneapolis, MN: Milkweed Editions.

Nachmias, C., and Palen, J. (1986). "Neighborhood satisfaction, expectations, and urban revitalization." *Journal of Urban Affairs* 8(4): 51–62.

Nager, A. R., and Wentworth, W. R. (1976). *Bryant Park: A comprehensive evaluation of its image and use with implications for urban open space design.* New York: Center for Human Environments, City University of New York.

Naimark, S. (1982). *A handbook of community gardening.* New York: Scribner.

Nasar, J. L. (1987). "Environmental correlates of evaluative appraisals of central business district scenes." *Landscape and Urban Planning* 14: 117–130.

Nasar, J. L. (1989). "Perception, cognition, and evaluation of urban places." In I. Altman and E. H. Zube (eds.), *Public places and spaces. New* York: Plenum Press, pp. 31–56.

Nasar, J. L. (1996). "Design in the context of fear: Increasing compatibility in difficult settings." In J. L. Nasar and B. B. Brown (eds.), *Public and private places: Proceedings of the twenty-seventh annual conference of the Environmental Design Research Association.* Edmund, OK: EDRA.

Nasar, J. L., and Fisher, B. (1993). "'Hot spots' of fear and crime: A multimethod investigation." *Journal of Environmental Psychology* 13: 187–206.

Nassauer, J. I. (1988a). "Landscape care: Perceptions of local people in landscape ecology and sustainable development." *Landscape and Land Use Planning* 8: 27–41.

Nassauer, J. I. (1988b). "The aesthetics of horticulture: Neatness as a form of care." *Hortscience* 23: 973–977.

Nassauer, J. I. (1993). "Ecological function and the perception of suburban residential landscapes." In P. H. Gobster (ed.), *Managing urban and high use recreation settings.* St. Paul, MN: USDA Forest Service, General Technical Report NC–163.

Nassauer, J. I. (1995a). "Culture and changing landscape structure." *Landscape Ecology* 10: 229–237.

Nassauer, J. I. (1995b). "Messy ecosystems, orderly frames." *Landscape Journal* 14(2): 161–170.

National Gardening Association. (1985). *Special report on community gardening in the U.S.* Burlington, VT: National Gardening Association.

National Park Service. (1995). *Heritage trails: Strengthening a regional community.* Denver, CO: Partnerships Branch, United States Department of Interior.

National Urban Forest Forum. (1988). *Shedding a few tears.* Washington, DC: American Forestry Association. January/February.

Neely, D., ed. (1994). *Social aspects of urban forestry.* (Journal of Arboriculture: A compendium, vol. 6). Savoy, IL: International Society of Arboriculture.

Newman, O. (1972). *Defensible space.* New York: Macmillan.

Newman, O. (1995). "Defensible space: A new physical planning tool for urban revitalization." *Journal of American Planning Association* 61(1): 149–155.

Nohl, W. (1984). "Traces of a participatory aesthetics in urban open spaces."

In D. Duerk and D. Cambell (eds.), *The challenge of diversity: Proceedings of the Environmental Design Research Association 15th Annual Conference.* San Luis Obispo: California Polytechnic State University, pp. 269.

O'Neill, M. J. (1991). "Effects of signage and floor plan configuration on wayfinding accuracy." *Environment and Behavior* 23: 553–574.

Owens, P. E. (1988). "Natural landscapes, gathering places and prospect refuge: Characteristics of outdoor places valued by teens." *Children's Environments Quarterly* 5: 17–24.

Passini, R. (1987). "Brain lesions and their effect on wayfinding: A review." In J. Harvey and D. Henning (eds.) *Public environments.* Washington, DC: Environmental Design Research Association, pp. 61–67.

Perkins, D. D.; Florin, P.; Rich, R. C.; and Wandersman, A. (1990). "Participation and the social and physical environment of residential blocks: Crime and community context." *Journal of Community Psychology* 18(1): 83–115.

Perkins, D. D.; Wandersman, A. H.; Abraham, H.; Rich, R. C.; and Taylor, R. B. (1993). "The physical environment of street crime: Defensible space, territoriality, and incivilities." *Journal of Environmental Psychology* 13(1): 29–49.

Peterson, G. L.; Dwyer, J. F.; and Darragh, A. J. (1983). "A behavioral urban recreation site choice model." *Leisure Sciences* 6(1): 61–81.

Petit, J., and Gangloff, D. (1995). "The megafauna: People of the urban ecosystem." *Urban Forests* 14: 10–17.

Pigram, J. J. (1993). "Human-nature relationships: Leisure environments and natural settings." In T. Gärling and R. G. Golledge (eds.), *Behavior and environment: Psychological and geographical approaches.* Amsterdam: Elsevier Science Publishers.

Platt, R. H.; Rowntree, R. A.; and Muick, P. C., eds. (1994). *The ecological city: Preserving and restoring urban diversity.* Amherst: University of Massachusetts Press.

Posner, M. I. (1973). *Cognition: An introduction.* Glenview, IL: Scott, Foresman.

Posner, M. I., and Keele, S. W. (1970). "Retention of abstract ideas." *Journal of Experimental Psychology* 83: 304.

Posner, M. I., and Rothbart, M. K. (1980). "The development of attentional mechanisms." In J. H. Flowers (ed.), *Nebraska symposium on motivation.* Lincoln: University of Nebraska Press.

Postman, N. (1985). *Amusing ourselves to death.* New York: Penguin Books.

Relf, D. (1992a). "Human issues in horticulture." *Hort Technology* 2(2): 159–171.

Relf, D. (1992b). The role of horticulture in human well-being and social development: A national symposium. Portland, OR: Timber Press.

Ruddell, E. J., and Hammitt, W. E. (1987). "Prospect refuge theory: A psychological orientation for edge effect in recreation environments." *Journal of Leisure Research* 19(4): 249–260.

Ryan, K. L., ed. (1993). *Trails for the twenty-first century: Planning, design, and management manual for multi-use trails.* Washington, DC: Island Press.

Ryan, R. L. (1995). *Perceptual river corridors: Understanding environmental preference in America's countryside.* Unpublished master's thesis, University of Michigan, Ann Arbor.

Sadalla, E. K., and Staplin, L. J. (1980). "An information model for distance cognition." *Environment and Behavior* 12: 183–193.

Schroeder, H. W. (1982). "Preferred features of urban parks and forests." *Journal of Arboriculture* 8: 317–322.

Schroeder, H. W. (1983). "Variations in the perception of urban forest recreation sites." *Leisure Sciences* 5(3): 221–230.

Schroeder, H. W. (1986). "Estimating park tree densities to maximize landscape esthetics." *Journal of Environmental Management* 23: 325–333.

Schroeder, H. W. (1988). "The experience of significant landscapes at Morton Arboretum." *Proceedings of the 1987 Society of American Foresters National Convention,* Minneapolis, October 18–21, 1987, pp. 378–381.

Schroeder, H. W. (1989). "Environment, behavior, and design research on urban forests." In E. H. Zube and G. T. Moore (eds.), *Advances in environment, behavior, and design,* vol. 2. New York: Plenum Press.

Schroeder, H. W. (1990). "Perceptions and preferences of urban forest users." *Journal of Arboriculture* 16(3): 58–61.

Schroeder, H. W. (in press). "Volunteers' motivations and values as reflected in ecosystem stewardship newsletters." *Proceedings of the 15th North American Prairie Conference.* St. Charles, Illinois, October 23–26, 1996.

Schroeder, H. W., and Anderson L. M. (1984). "Perception of personal safety in urban recreation sites." *Journal of Leisure Research* 16: 178–194.

Schroeder, H.W.; Buhyoff, G. J.; and Cannon, W. N., Jr. (1986). "Cross-validation of predictive models for aesthetic quality of residential streets." *Journal of Environmental Management* 23: 309–316.

Schroeder, H. W., and Cannon, W. N., Jr. (1983). "The aesthetic contribution of trees to residential streets in Ohio towns." *Journal of Arboriculture* 9: 237–243.

Schroeder, H. W., and Green, T. L. (1985). "Public preference for tree density in a municipal forest program." *Journal of Arboriculture* 11: 272–277.

Schroeder, H. W., and Ruffolo, S. R. (1996). "Householder evaluations of street trees in a Chicago suburb." *Journal of Arboriculture* 22(1): 35–43.

Shaffer, G. S., and Anderson, L. M. (1985). "Perceptions of the security and attractiveness of urban parking lots." *Journal of Environmental Psychology* 5: 311–323.

Shaw, W. W.; Mangun, W. R.; and Lyons, J. R. (1985). "Residential enjoyment of wildlife resources by Americans." *Leisure Sciences* 7: 361–375.

Sheets, V. L., and Manzer, C. D. (1991). "Affect, cognition, and urban vegetation: Some effects of adding trees along city streets." *Environment and Behavior* 23: 285–304.

Simmons, D. A. (1994). "Urban children's preferences for nature: Lessons for environmental education." *Children's Environments* 11: 194–203.

Skelton, R. (1994). "Harlem green-aissance." *Amicus Journal* (Fall): pp. 14–17.

Spotts, D. M., and Stynes, D. J. (1984). "Public awareness and knowledge of urban parks: A case study." *Journal of Park and Recreation Administration* 2: 1–12.

Spotts, D. M., and Stynes, D. J. (1985). "Measuring the public's familiarity with recreation areas." *Journal of Leisure Research* 17: 253–265.

Stankey, G. H. (1989). "Solitude for the multitudes." In I. Altman and E. H. Zube (eds.), *Public places and spaces*. New York: Plenum Press, pp. 277–299.

Stewart, J., and McKenzie, R. L. (1978). "Composing urban spaces for security, privacy, and outlook." *Landscape Architecture* 68: 392–398.

Stoks, F. (1983). "Assessing urban environments for danger of violent crime: Especially rape." In D. Joiner, G. Brimilcombe, J. Daish, J. Gray, and D. Kernohan (eds.), *Proceedings of the Conference on People and Physical Environment Research*. Wellington, New Zealand: Ministry of Works and Development.

Sullivan, W. C. (1994). "Perceptions of the rural-urban fringe: Citizen preferences for natural and developed settings." *Landscape and Urban Planning* 29: 85–101.

Sullivan, W. C. (1996). "Cluster housing at the rural-urban fringe: The search for adequate and satisfying places to live." *Journal of Architectural and Planning Research* 13(4): 291–309.

Sullivan, W. C., and Kuo, F. E. (1996). *Do trees strengthen urban communities, reduce domestic violence?* Atlanta, GA: USDA Forest Service, Forestry Report no. R8–FR 56.

Sullivan, W. C.; Kuo, F. E.; and Prabhu, M. (1996). "Assessing the impact of environmental impact statements on citizens." *Environmental Impact Assessment Review* 16(3): 171–182.

Sullivan, W. C.; Kuo, F. E.; and Prabhu, M. (1997). "Communicating with citizens: The power of photosimulations and simple-editing." *Environmental Impact Assessment Review* 17(3): 295–310.

Talbot, J., and Frost, J. L. (1989). "Magical playscapes." *Childhood Education* 66: 11–19.

Talbot, J. F. (1982). "Zoning reconsidered: The impacts of environmental aesthetics in urban neighborhoods." In P. Bart, A. Chen, and G. Francescato (eds.), *Proceedings of EDRA 13: Knowledge for Design*. Washington, DC: Environmental Design and Research Association.

Talbot, J. F. (1988). "Planning concerns relating to urban nature settings: The role of size and other physical features." In J. L. Nasar (ed.), *Environmental aesthetics: Theory, research, and applications*. Cambridge: Cambridge University Press.

Talbot, J. F. (1993). "Public participation in rail-trail planning: Two case studies." In P. H. Gobster (ed.), *Managing urban and high use recreation settings*. St. Paul, MN: USDA Forest Service, General Technical Report NC–163.

Talbot, J. F., and Bardwell, L. V. (1989). "Making 'open spaces' that work: Research and guidelines for natural areas in medium-density housing." In G. Hardie, R. Moore, and H. Sanoff (eds.), *Changing paradigms*. Oklahoma City: Environmental Design Research Association, pp. 110–115.

Talbot, J. F.; Bardwell, L. V.; and Kaplan, R. (1987). "The functions of urban nature: Uses and values of different types of urban nature settings." *Journal of Architecture and Planning Research* 4: 47–63.

Talbot, J. F., and Kaplan, R. (1984). "Needs and fears: The response to trees and nature in the inner city." *Journal of Arboriculture* 10(8): 222–228.

Talbot, J. F., and Kaplan, R. (1986). "Judging the sizes of urban open areas: Is bigger always better?" *Landscape Journal* 5: 83–92.

Talbot, J. F., and Kaplan, R. (1991). "The benefits of nearby nature for elderly apartment residents." *International Journal of Aging and Human Development* 33: 119–130.

Talbot, J. F., and Kaplan, R. (1993). "Preferences for nearby nature settings: Ethnic and age variations." In P. Gobster (ed.), *Managing urban and high-use recreation settings.* St. Paul, MN: USDA Forest Service, General Technical Report NC–163.

Talbot, J. F.; Kaplan, R.; Kuo, F. E.; and Kaplan, S. (1993). "Factors that enhance effectiveness of visitor maps." *Environment and Behavior* 25: 743–760.

Taylor, A. F.; Wiley, A.; Kuo, F. E.; and Sullivan, W. C. (1998). "Growing up in the inner city: Green spaces as places to grow." *Environment and Behavior* 30(1): 3–27.

Tennessen, C. M., and Cimprich, B. E. (1995). "Views to nature: Affects of attention." *Journal of Environmental Psychology* 15(1): 77–85.

Trent, R. B.; Neumann. E.; and Alon, K. (1986). "Presentation mode and question format artifacts in visual assessment research." *Landscape and Urban Planning* 14: 225–235.

Tyznik, A. (1981). "Trees as design elements in the landscape." *Journal of Arboriculture* 72: 53–55.

Ulrich, R. S. (1979). "Visual landscapes and psychological well-being." *Landscape Research* 4: 17–19.

Ulrich, R. S. (1981). "Natural versus urban scenes: Some psychological effects." *Environment and Behavior* 13: 523–556.

Ulrich, R. S. (1984). "View through a window may influence recovery from surgery." *Science* 224: 420–421.

Ulrich, R. S. (1986). "Human responses to vegetation and landscape." *Landscape and Urban Planning* 13: 29–44.

Ulrich, R. S., and Addoms, D. L. (1981). "Psychological and recreational benefits of a residential park." *Journal of Leisure Research* 13: 43–65.

Ulrich, R. S.; Lunden, O.; and Eltinge, J. L. (1996). "Effects of viewing nature and abstract pictures on heart surgery patients." In J. L. Nasar and B. B. Brown (eds.), *Public and private places: Proceedings of the twenty-seventh annual conference of the Environmental Design Research Association.* Edmund, OK: EDRA

Ulrich, R. S., and Simmons, R. F. (1986). "Recovery from stress during exposure to everyday outdoor environments." In *Proceedings of EDRA 17.* Washington, DC: Environmental Design and Research Association.

Vachta, K. E., and McDonough, M. H. (1996). "Applications of social forestry in the urban United States: Community outcomes of the urban resources initiative in Detroit." *Proceedings of the Sixth International Symposium on Society and Resource Management.* University Park, Pennsylvania State University, pp. 185–186.

Verderber, S. (1982). "Designing for the therapeutic functions of windows in the hospital environment." In P. Bart, et al. (eds.), *Knowledge in design.* Washington DC: Environmental Design Research Association, pp. 476–492.

Verderber, S. (1986). "Dimensions of person-window transactions in the hospital environment." *Environment and Behavior* 18: 450–466.

Verderber, S., and Reuman, D. (1987). "Windows, views, and health status in hospital therapeutic environments." *Journal of Architectural and Planning Research* 4: 120–133.

Vitz, P. C. (1990). "The use of stories in moral development: New psychological reasons for an old education method." *American Psychologist* 45: 709–720.

Wandersman, A. (1979). "User participation: A study of types of participation, effects, mediators, and individual differences." *Environment and Behavior* 11(2): 185–208.

Wandersman, A. (1987). "Research on citizen participation." *Participation Network* 5: 22–25.

Warren, D. H. (1994). "Self-localization on plan and oblique maps." *Environment and Behavior* 26: 71–98.

Warren, D. H., and Scott, T. E. (1993). "Map alignment in traveling multi-segment routes." *Environment and Behavior* 25: 643–666.

Weber, W.W. (1980). *Comparison of media for public participation in natural environmental planning.* Unpublished doctoral dissertation, University of Michigan, Ann Arbor.

Wecker, S. C. (1964). "Habitat selection." *Scientific American* 211 (4): 109–116.

Weisman, J. (1981). "Evaluating architectural legibility: Way-finding in the built environment." *Environment and Behavior* 13(2): 189–204.

Wendling, R. C. (1980). "Black/white differences in outdoor recreation behavior: State-of-the-art and recommendations for management and research." *Social Research in National Parks and Wildlands Areas: Proceedings of the Conference.* Gatlinburg, Tennessee, March 21–22, 1980.

West, M. J. (1986). *Landscape views and stress responses in the prison environment.* Unpublished master's thesis, University of Washington, Seattle.

Westover, T. N. (1985a) "Perceptions of crime and safety in three midwestern parks." *Professional Geographer* 37(4): 410–420.

Westover, T. N. (1985b). "Perceptions of rule compliance and law enforcement in urban and suburban parks." *Recreation Research Review* 12(2): 22–29.

Westover, T. N. (1986). "Park use and perception: Gender differences." *Journal of Park and Recreation Administration* 4(2): 1–8.

Westphal, L. M. (1993). "Why trees? Urban forestry volunteers values and motivations." In P. H. Gobster (ed.), *Managing urban and high use recreation settings.* St. Paul, MN: USDA Forest Service, General Technical Report NC–163, pp. 19–23.

Westphal, L. M., and Childs, G. (1994). "Overcoming obstacles: Creating volunteer partnerships." *Journal of Forestry* 92(10): 28–32.

Westphal, L. M., and Lieber, S. R. (1986). "Predicting the effect of alternative trail design on visitor satisfaction in park settings." *Landscape Journal* 5(1): 39–44.

Wiedermann, D. (1985). "How secure are public open spaces?" *Garden and Landschaft* 95: 26–27.

Wiberg-Carlson, D., and Schroeder, H. W. (1992). *Modeling and mapping urban bicyclists preferences for trail environments*. St. Paul, MN: USDA Forest Service, Research Paper NC–303.

Wisner, B.; Stea, D.; and Kruks, S. (1994). "Participatory and action research methods." In E. H. Zube and G. T. Moore (eds.), *Advances in environment, behavior, and design*, vol. 3. New York: Plenum Press.

Wohlwill, J. F. (1976). "Environmental aesthetics: The environment as a source of affect." In I. Altman and J. F. Wohlwill (eds.), *Human behavior and environment: Advances in theory and research*, vol. 1. New York: Plenum Press, pp. 37–86.

Wohlwill, J. F. (1983). "The concept of nature: A psychologist's view." In I. Altman and J. F. Wohlwill (eds.), *Behavior and the natural environment*. New York: Plenum Press, pp. 5–37.

Wohlwill, J. F., and Harris, G. (1980). "Response to congruity or contrast for man-made features in natural recreation settings." *Leisure Sciences* 3(4): 349–365.

Wolf, K. L. (1993). *Shoreline residential development: Landscape management alternatives and public preference*. Unpublished doctoral dissertation, University of Michigan, Ann Arbor.

Woodcock, D. M. (1982). *A functionalist approach to environmental preference*. Unpublished doctoral dissertation, University of Michigan, Ann Arbor.

Yang, B. E. (1988). *A cross-cultural comparison for Korean, Japanese, and western landscape styles*. Unpublished doctoral dissertation, University of Michigan, Ann Arbor.

Yang, B. E., and Brown, T. J. (1992). "A cross-cultural comparison of preferences for landscape styles and landscape elements." *Environment and Behavior* 24: 471–507.

Yang, B. E., and Kaplan, R. (1990). "The perception of landscape style: A cross-cultural comparison." *Landscape and Urban Planning* 19: 251–262.

Young, R. A., and Flowers, M. L. (1982). *Users of an urban natural area: Their characteristics, use patterns, satisfactions, and recommendations*. Forestry research report 82–4. University of Illinois, Urbana-Champaign: Department of Forestry, Agricultural Experiment Station.

Yu, K. (1995). "Cultural variations in landscape preference: Comparisons among Chinese subgroups and Western design experts." *Landscape and Urban Planning* 32: 107–126.

Zube, E. H. (1978). "The natural history of urban trees." In S. Kaplan and R. Kaplan (eds.), *Humanscape: Environments for people*. Belmont, CA: Duxbury. (Republished by Ulrich's, Ann Arbor, MI: 1982.)

Photo Credits

The photographs included in the book came from many sources. Unless otherwise noted, the photograph was taken by Robert L. Ryan, who is also responsible for all the sketches.

Many thanks to the following individuals and organizations for permission to include photographs or graphic material:

Maureen E. Austin (photograph on p. 160).

City of Ann Arbor, Michigan, Solid Waste Department (figures on p. 141).

Creekside Master's Project, University of Michigan: David R. Barnes (left photograph in figure on p. 126); Kenneth J. Polakowski (top left photograph in figure on p. 138); and Sarah H. Weiss (figures on pp. 134 and 139).

Howard Deardorff (figure on p. 128).

Dan DeWald, City of Bellevue, Washington, Parks and Community Services Department (figures on p. 33 and bottom of p. 47).

Bruce Dvorak and William Sullivan (figure on p. 130).

Donna L. Erikson (figure at the bottom of p. 135).

Bob Grese (right photograph on p. 126, and figure on p. 137).

Abram W. Kaplan (top row and bottom right photographs on p. 112, middle right photograph in figure at the top of p. 135 used in the North Main project).

Michigan State University, Cooperative Extension Service (right bulletin in figure at the top of p. 140).

Kenneth Polakowski (left photograph in center figure on p. 94).

University of Michigan Nichols Arboretum Photo File (figure on p. 136 by Guerin Wilkinson, and bottom left photograph in figure on p. 138).

John A. Witter (left bulletin in figure at the top p. 140).

Many of the photographs were taken for research purposes, over a period of several decades. The following photographs were taken as part of projects that received funding from USDA, North Central Forest Experiment Station,* through numerous Cooperative Agreements: left photograph in figure on p. 11; top figure

---

* Where it is possible, the photographer is identified.

on p. 12; bottom left photo on p. 12 (Abram W. Kaplan); middle photograph in figure on p. 38 (Stephen Kaplan); top figure on p. 47; right photo in figure on p. 103; figure on p. 115; top side-by-side photographs in the middle of p. 117 (Janet F. Talbot); right photograph in figure at the bottom of p. 117; figure on p. 118; and bottom right photograph in figure at the top of p. 133 (Abram W. Kaplan).

The following photographs were included in other research projects.* North Main project: right photograph in figure at the bottom of p. 38; right photograph in figure p. 93; left photograph in figure at the bottom of p. 114; bottom right photograph in figure on p. 120; and photographs in figure at the top of p. 135. Liberty Plaza project: figure on p. 132 (Terry J. Brown). Swift Run Drain project: figure on p. 36 (Stephen Kaplan); left photograph in figure at the bottom of p. 38; and top photograph in figure in the middle of p. 114. Model study: figure at the top of p. 129 (Stephen Kaplan).

Stephen Kaplan took the following photographs: figure at the bottom of p. 12 (right), figure on p. 40, figure on p. 41, figure on p. 43, figure on p. 45, figure on p. 75 (left), figure on p. 76, p. 78 (bottom), figure on p. 83, figure at the top of p. 84 (left), figure in the middle of p. 94 (right), left figure on p. 103, middle figure on p. 104, figure at the top of p. 116 (left), figure at the bottom of p. 117 (left), figure on p. 119, figure at the bottom of p. 133 (bottom right), and top figure on p. 138.

* Where it is possible, the photographer is identified.

Index

Administrative work, 4, 136
Aesthetics, 10–16, 26, 140–142
Alternatives, in design, 132–133, 159, 165
Animals, 20, 21, 32, 69, 97, 113
Anxiety. *See* Fear
Apartment communities, 33, 101, 137
Assessment. *See* Feedback; Tracking
Attention/comprehension capabilities, 17–18, 22–23, 62
  effect of restorative environments on, 67–68
  separation from distractions and, 73, 156, 164
  views and, 103–104, 153, 165
"Away," concept of, 18–19, 20, 71, 155, 156

Benches, 70, 75, 97
Big spaces. *See* Open/undifferentiated areas
Blocked views, 11–12, 16, 33–34, 39, 93, 111
Boardwalks, 94
Book, how to use, 5–6
Boundaries. *See* Ownership, sense of; Partitions
Bridges, 70, 95
Brochures, 139–142, 151, 165
Buildings, 21, 33. *See also* Courtyards; Windows
  labels and symbols for, 62
  nature centers in, 107, 108
  views and, 103, 104, 105, 108

Children, 56, 138
Choice points, 53, 58, 79–80, 81, 150, 153
Choices, in design, 132–133, 159, 165
Coherence
  gateways and, 81
  information on the environment and, 13, 14, 15, 16, 150

of paths and signs, 55–56
  preference and, 40–41, 102, 163
  regions and, 51, 150
Color, use of, 55, 69, 72
Comfort, 31, 32, 35–36, 42, 89, 130, 152. *See also* Restorative environments
Community. *See* People; Public
Compatibility, 21, 152
Complexity, 13, 14–15, 16, 39, 57–58, 60–61, 100
Conflict resolution, 27, 127
Courtyards, 105, 107, 108, 119
Cultural differences, 25

Decision points. *See* Choice points
Depth, sense of, 46, 71–72, 101, 154, 156, 163
Design, 79, 121
  engaging people in, 125, 126–135, 158–159, 165
  information sharing and, 22–27
  of Japanese gardens, 72
  in way-finding, 50, 51–56, 163
Distraction, separation from, 73–74, 156, 164

Ecological aspects, 2, 4, 93, 94, 109, 121
Ecological restoration, 4
Economic aspects, 22, 128
Education of the public, 2, 4, 23–24
Enclosure, sense of, 6, 73, 74, 110, 116, 117, 119–120, 165. *See also* Small spaces
Enjoyment of natural environment, 17–22
Entrances. *See* Gateways
Experiments, small, 6, 143–145, 160, 161, 165
Expertise, 25–27, 28, 124, 140, 141
Exploration, 8–16, 28
  familiarity with place and, 109
  framework for, 10–13, 16

Exploration (*continued*)
  gateways and, 81
  with mobility limitations, 28, 56
  mystery and, 43–45, 154
  need for, 31, 89
  openings and, 48
  patterns of, 153–155
  possibilities of. *See* Maps
  preference and, 39–49
  providing opportunities for, 153–155
  readings, 170–171
  sense of depth and, 46, 154
  site field trips, 130–131
  smooth ground and, 42
  views and, 100, 105, 153, 154–155,
    165
Extent, sense of, 19–20, 71–72, 73,
    101–102, 155, 156, 164, 165

Familiarity, 31, 35–36, 130, 152, 163
Farmland, 11
Fascination, quiet, 17, 18, 20–21, 69–70,
    105, 156, 164
Fatigue. *See* Mental fatigue
Fear, 6, 29, 32, 163
  familiarity and, 35–36, 152
  of getting lost, 46, 49, 95. *See also*
    Legibility
  mental fatigue and, 17
  need for exploration and, 31, 89
  perceived *vs.* real, 32, 35
  preferences and, 31–48, 163
  readings, 175–178
  upsetting information, 25, 62
  visual access and, 31, 32, 33–34, 153
  way-finding confidence and, 32
Feedback, 66, 134–135, 158, 159, 164,
    165
Fences, 37–38, 83, 84
  coherence and, 40, 41
  in Japanese gardens, 72
  materials for, 75
  peepholes in, 106
Field trips, 130–131
Finding the way. *See* Way-finding
Flora. *See* Gardens; Trees; Vegetation

Gardening, 21, 69
Gardens, 20, 39, 72, 110, 115, 119, 138,
    160

Gateways, 6, 81–87
  as choice points, 79–80, 81
  definition, 81
  need for partitions, 83–84, 164
  orientation and, 81, 85, 153, 164
  readings, 185
  view through, 86–87, 107, 154, 164
Golf course view, 101, 102
Grassroots efforts, 124, 138
Ground texture, 12, 40, 41, 42, 152, 163

Health, effect of restorative environments
    on, 68
Hedges, 40, 43, 81, 120
Historical aspects, 98, 123
Human characteristics, 7–28
Human sign, 37–38, 46, 53, 54, 98, 103,
    104, 152, 163

Image of the City, 49
Imagination. *See* Mind's eye; Mystery
Information
  environment as a source of, 9–10,
    103–104, 151, 153, 165
  level of complexity, 140
  new, incorporation of, 23–24, 58
  promise of. *See* Mystery
  psychological costs of managing, 8,
    16–22
  quantity *vs.* quality, 25, 57–58, 60–61,
    95, 130, 139, 140, 151, 165
  readings, 170–175
  role in human psyche, 9, 139–142
  sharing of, 8, 22–27, 28, 145, 172–175
  understanding and exploration, 8–16
  understanding and participation, 123,
    124, 128–131, 139–142, 158, 165
  upsetting, 25, 62
Intuition, 3, 4

Labels, 62–64, 151
Landmarks, 15, 55, 150
  gateways and partitions as, 81
  historical, 98
  on maps, 58, 61, 63
  openings as, 48
  sense of depth and, 46, 154
  on trails, for orientation, 95, 96,
    97–98, 150
  in way-finding design, 50, 53–54, 163

Landscape architecture, 4, 76–77
Landscapes. *See also* Open/undiffer-
    entiated areas
  densely vegetated with obstructed view,
    11–12, 16, 33–34, 39, 93, 111
  perception of regions in, 51–52
Lawns, 37, 38, 101, 116
Legibility
  information on the environment and,
    13, 15, 16
  large mowed areas and, 116
  of openings, 48, 152
  of open spaces, 39
  partitions and, 81
  sense of depth and, 46, 154
  views and, 100
Light, quality of, 20, 39, 44, 48, 103,
    111
Locomotion, 31, 39, 42, 47, 89–98,
    185–186. *See also* Paths; Trails
Lookouts. *See* Overlooks
Lost, getting, 46, 49, 95. *See also*
    Way-finding

Management, 79, 121
  comfort in human sign, 37–38, 152
  engaging people in, 125, 136–145,
    158, 165
  information sharing and, 22–27
  small experiments in, 143–145,
    160–161, 165
Man-made elements. *See* Human sign
Maps. *See also* Models, site
  accuracy *vs.* alienation, 57–58, 60–61,
    95, 151, 164
  alignment of north, 65, 151, 164
  bird's eye view *vs.* oblique view, 61
  design of, 50, 51–56, 59, 164
  feedback on, 66, 158, 164
  labels and symbols, 62–64, 151, 164
  orientation from, 57–59, 60, 150, 164
  points of interest, 62–64, 97–98, 164
  portable, 49
  posted, 49
  use of shading, 59
  way-finding patterns, 50, 57–66, 158,
    164
Materials, 75, 94, 95, 152, 164
Matrix of patterns and themes, 4, 122,
    163–165

Media, 136
Meetings. *See* Public hearings
Mental fatigue, 17, 18–22, 28, 156. *See
    also* Restorative environments
Mind's eye, mapping for the, 23–24,
    60–61, 154–155, 165
Models, site, 128, 129, 130, 134, 135
Mowed areas, 37, 38, 101, 116
Mystery
  of fog, 39, 44
  gateways and, 82, 86–87, 154
  information on the environment and,
    13, 16
  large mowed areas and, 116
  of openings, 48, 152
  preference and, 39, 43–45, 154, 163
  of small spaces, 71–72, 155, 156, 157
  views and, 100, 105, 165

Natural environment
  contact with. *See* Trails
  effects of isolation from the, 29
  effects of people on the, 2, 93, 109
  factors in enjoyment of, 17–22
  familiarity and perception of, 36, 152
  framework for preferences, 10–13, 16,
    29–30
  "nearby nature," 147–148
  size and restorative properties, 67
  as source of information, 9–10,
    103–104, 151, 153, 165
  use of term, 1
Natural resources, 4
Nature
  importance of, 168–170
  "nearby," 147–148, 169–170
  use of term, 1
Nature centers, 107, 108
Negotiation, 27, 127
North, map alignment of, 65, 151
Notices, 139–142, 151, 165

Obstructed view, 11–12, 16, 33–34, 39,
    93, 111
Openings, 47–48, 53, 152, 163
Open/undifferentiated areas, 11, 39, 52,
    101
  as an element of place, 109, 110,
    115–116, 157, 165
  small experiments in, 143, 161

Orientation to the environment
exploration and, 153
gateways and, 81, 85, 153, 164
path of trail and, 95–96, 150
understanding and, 150
way-finding maps, 49, 57–59, 60, 164
"Outside" *vs.* "inside." *See* Gateways
Overhead areas, 42, 73, 119
Overlooks, 5–6, 34, 93, 99, 103–104,
107, 108, 155. *See also* Views and
vistas
Ownership, sense of, 109, 115, 117,
136–137. *See also* Participation

Pamphlets, 139–142, 151, 165
Parking areas, screening of, 108
Parks, 4, 29, 115, 138, 143–144,
160–161
Participation, 6
in design, 123–135, 151
in management, 136–146, 158, 165
Partitions, 81, 83–84, 106, 119, 164,
185
Paths, 40, 41, 42. *See also* Locomotion;
Trails
choice points, as landmarks, 53, 58
in Japanese gardens, 72
maps and orientation, 57–59, 60, 151
primary and secondary, 55
in way-finding design, 50, 55–56, 151,
163
width of, 55, 91, 92, 95
winding quality of, 16, 43, 91, 116,
154
Patterns
engaging people in design, 125,
158–159, 164
engaging people in management, 125,
159, 165
of exploration, 153–155, 164
format of, 30
of gateways and partitions, 81, 82,
107, 164
of places, 109–110, 165
of public participation, 158–159, 165
of restorative environments, 67, 68,
156–157, 164
of small experiments, 160, 165
and themes, matrix, 4, 122, 163–165
of trails, 89, 90, 107, 164

understanding the environment,
150–152
use of intuition with, 3
use of term, 3–4, 5, 30
of views and vistas, 99, 100, 154–155,
165
of way-finding, 49, 50, 163–164
People. *See also* Public
diversity of, 148
engaging, 122, 123–145, 165,
189–193
evidence of. *See* Human sign
overcoming difficulty in working with,
148–161
Personalization of space, 117, 138
Photographs, 129, 133, 134, 135,
217–218
Picnic areas, 40, 115, 133
Place, sense of
enclosure as an element, 110, 117,
119–120, 165
open/undifferentiated areas and, 109,
110, 115–116, 157, 165
patterns, 156–157, 165
readings, 186–189
small spaces and, 109, 110, 117–118,
157, 165
trees as an element, 109, 110,
111–112, 156, 165
water as an element, 109, 110,
113–114, 156, 165
Plants. *See* Gardens; Trees; Vegetation
Points of interest, 62–64, 97–98, 164
Preference, 10–13, 29–30, 39–48, 163
elements of, 6, 10–13
fear and, 31–48
gateways/partitions and, 81
large mowed areas and, 116
matrix, 13
readings, 178–180
trails and, 89, 93, 150, 153
trees and, 111, 156
views and, 100
Privacy, 119
Psychological aspects. *See also* Extent,
sense of; Fascination, quiet
aesthetics of a view, 10–16, 99,
103–104, 105, 154–155, 165
compatibility, 21, 152
costs of managing information, 16–22

effect of isolation from nature, 29
effect of restorative environments on, 67–68
fear, perceived *vs.* real, 32, 35
human bias in understanding information, 152
incorporation of new information, 23–24, 60–61, 171–172
mapping for the mind's eye, 60–61
mental fatigue, 17, 18–22, 28, 156
separation from distraction, 73–74, 156, 164
views and imagination, 99–100, 105, 154–155, 165
Public. *See also* Visitors
  diversity of, 148
  education of, 2, 4, 23–24
  input by the, 22–23
  multiple views of the, 124–125, 127, 131
  overcoming difficulty in working with, 148–161
  preference for places, 10–13, 29–30
  as source of feedback, 134–135, 159, 165
  stewardship and volunteerism, 4, 112, 136, 137
  vs. "experts," 4, 124
Public hearings, 124, 135
Public officials, 127
Public participation
  in design, 123–135, 151, 158–159
  in management, 136–145, 158, 165
  patterns, 158–159
  readings, 189–193
  representatives for, 135
  small experiments in, 143–145, 160–161, 165

Quality assessment. *See* Feedback; Tracking
Quiet fascination. *See* Fascination, quiet

Recreational sports, 21, 69, 89, 113, 132, 133
Regions
  number of, 52
  partitions for, 83–84, 104
  understanding the environment and, 150

use in big spaces, 115, 116, 157
use in small spaces, 72
in views, 103–104
in way-finding design, 50, 51–52, 150, 163
in way-finding maps, 58–59
Restoration. *See* Ecological restoration; Restorative environments
Restorative environments, 6, 28, 29, 40, 67–80. *See also* Benches; Overlooks; Points of interest
  characteristics of, 18–22, 147
  patterns of, 156–157, 164
  readings, 182–184
  windows as, 18–19, 70, 76–78, 99, 156, 164
Roadways, 101, 118

Scale, effect on diversity and richness, 15
Seasonal aspects, 20, 69, 70, 72, 112
Shelters, 21, 53, 133
Shrubs, 33–34, 119. *See also* Vegetation
Signs, 9, 49
  at gateways, 85
  orientation *vs.* distraction, 96
  at path intersections, 53
  in way-finding design, 50, 55–56, 151, 163
Site models. *See* Models, site
Small experiments, 6, 143–145, 160, 161, 165
Small spaces
  as an element of place, 109, 110, 117–118, 157, 165
  sense of enclosure in, 73–74, 117, 119, 156, 165
  sense of extent in, 71–72, 155, 156, 164
Smooth ground, 42, 152, 163
Solitude, 109, 119
Steps, materials for, 75
Stewardship, 112, 123, 125, 136
Structures. *See* Buildings; Shelters
Symbols, 5, 62–64, 128, 151

Territory. *See* Ownership, sense of
Texture. *See also* Ground texture
  in Japanese gardens, 72
  of paths, 55
  sense of enclosure and, 73

Texture (*continued*)
  use in small spaces, 72
  of water's edge, 113, 114, 156
Themes, 5–6, 28
  major, 148–149
  patterns and, matrix of, 4, 122,
    163–165
Topography, 46, 61, 101, 154
Tracking, during public participation,
    144–145
Trails, 6, 80, 133
  for commuting, 89
  following. *See* Way-finding
  grooming of, 34, 37, 38
  interpretive, 35
  layout, 95–96
  locomotion and, 89–98, 164
  maintenance of, 138
  narrow and curving, 91–92, 154, 164
  readings, 185–186
  self-guided, 35
  smooth ground along, 42, 152
  surface of, 94, 95, 152, 164
  understanding the environment and,
    150
  view from, 93, 107, 153, 164
Tree-planting projects, 112, 124, 138
Trees, 80. *See also* Vegetation
  as an element of place, 109, 110,
    111–112, 156, 165
  coherence and, 41
  groves, 133
  as landmarks, 53, 97
  mystery of, 43, 44, 45
  obstruction of view by, 11–12, 33–34,
    93
  openings in, 47–48
  pruning, 33–34
  role and functions of, 76, 111, 112,
    119
  row of, 12, 81, 83, 84, 104, 119, 120

Underbrush, 33–34, 119
Understanding information
  human bias in, 152
  during public participation, 123, 124,
    128–131, 139–142, 151, 158, 165
  readings, 170–171
Understanding the environment, 8–16
  framework for, 10–13, 16

patterns of, 150–152
preference and, 39–49
readings, 170–171

Vandalism, 37–38
Vegetation, 20. *See also* Gardens; Trees
  adjacent to paths, 55
  adjacent to roads, 101
  adjacent to water, 113–114, 156
  cutting/thinning of, 33
  public participation experiments with,
    143–145, 160–161
  as screen for undesirable views, 34,
    102, 108
  similarity of, and coherence, 40–41
  view obstructed by, 11–12, 16, 33–34,
    39, 93, 111
Viewing points. *See* Overlooks
Views and vistas, 6, 99–108. *See also*
    Openings; Overlooks; Visual
    access
  artificial, 106
  effects of expertise on aesthetics, 25–27
  exploration and, 100, 105, 153,
    154–155, 165
  in Japanese gardens, 72
  map orientation aligned with, 65
  obstructed, 11, 12, 16, 33–34, 39, 93,
    111
  opportunities to provide, 106–108,
    155, 165
  partial. *See* Mystery
  readings, 186
  through gateways, 86–87, 154, 164
  from the trail, 93, 107, 153
  two-dimensional *vs.* three-dimensional,
    13, 105
  undesirable, 34
  use of enclosures in, 74
  vertical, 105
Visitor centers, 33
Visitors
  new *vs.* repeat, 25–27, 36, 55, 153
  as source of feedback, 66, 134–135,
    158, 159, 165
Vistas. *See* Overlooks; Views and vistas
Visual access, 31, 32, 33–34, 102, 153,
    163. *See also* Openings; Views
    and vistas
Volunteers, 4, 136, 137

Walls, 37–38, 83
Water, 69, 70, 80
    as an element of place, 109, 110,
        113–114, 156, 165
    edge of, 113–114, 156
    gateways to, 86
    polluted, 113
    trails near, 92, 93
    vegetation around, 104
    waterfalls as landmarks, 96
Way-finding, 30, 49–66. *See also* Maps;
        Signs
    confidence in, 32
    design, 50, 51–56, 163
    getting lost, 46, 49, 95

    legibility and, 15
    maps, 50, 57–66, 158, 164
    readings, 180–182
Wheelchair access, 28, 56
Width of trail, 55, 91, 92, 95, 154
Wildlife, 21, 69, 97, 108, 113
Windows, 107
    artificial, 106
    small spaces and, 117
    as sources of restoration, 18–19, 70,
        76–78, 99, 156, 164
    vertical views from, 105

Zoos, 19, 20, 21